THE WHITE STAR COLLECTION

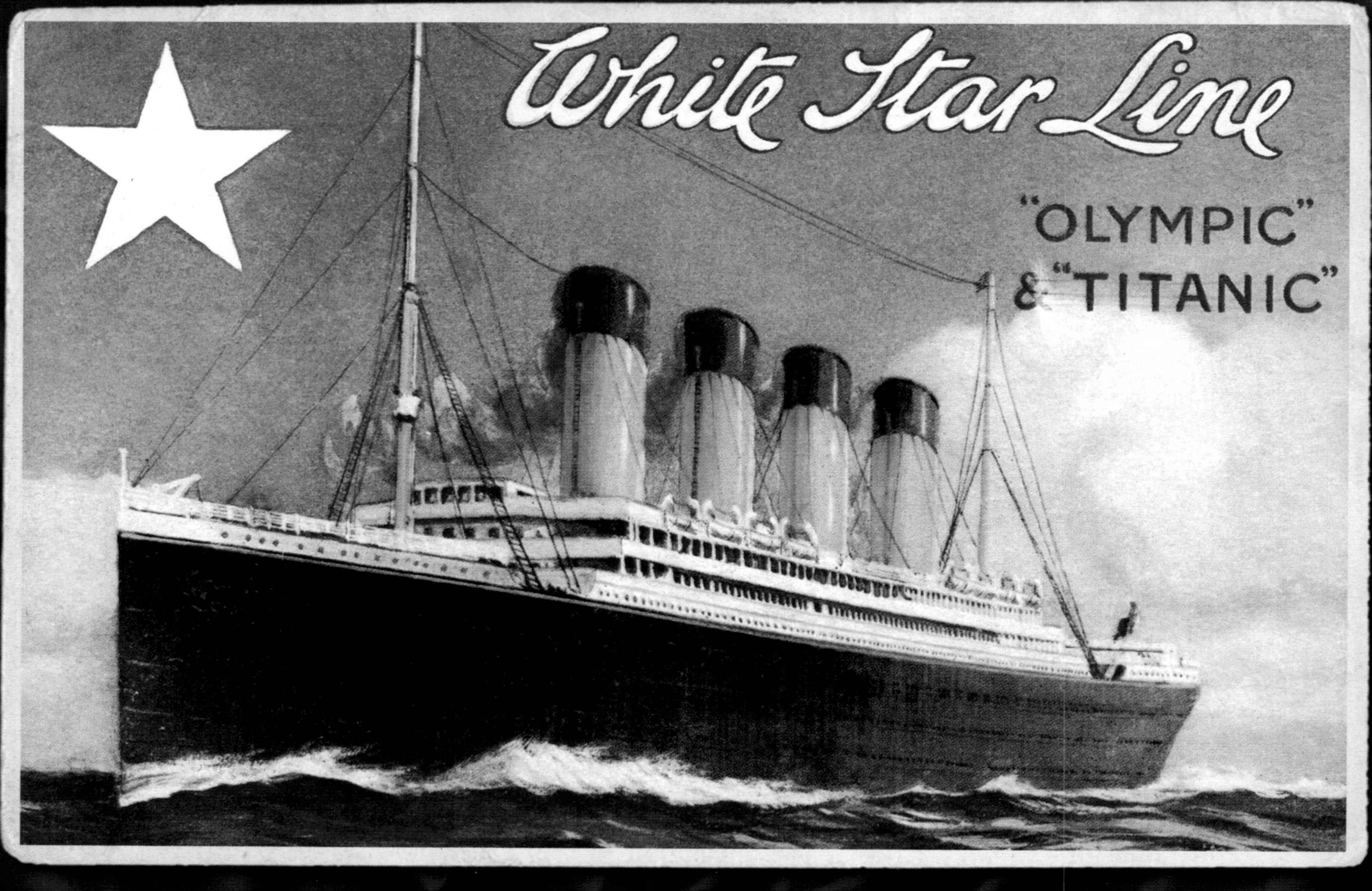
White Star Line
"OLYMPIC"
& "TITANIC"

THE WHITE STAR COLLECTION

A SHIPPING LINE IN POSTCARDS

PATRICK MYLON

The
History
Press ▸

To Thomas Henry Ismay (1837–99),

the founder of the Oceanic Steam Navigation Company

(The White Star Line)

First published 2011

The History Press
The Mill, Brimscombe Port
Stroud, Gloucestershire, GL5 2QG
www.thehistorypress.co.uk

British Library Cataloguing in Publication Data.
A catalogue record for this book is available from the British Library.

isbn 978 0 7524 5937 0

Typesetting and origination by The History Press
Production managed by Jellyfish Print Solutions and manufactured in India

CONTENTS

INTRODUCTION

I first began collecting postcards, featuring the White Star Line and its vessels, in the early 1980s but it was much later that I became aware of the wealth of history and information carried on their reverse.

This book is not a history of the White Star Line, nor does it attempt to feature all the vessels owned and operated by the company. In many cases I found several cards featuring the same vessel each of which told a different story. Some ships are covered only briefly, primarily because I could not find sufficiently interesting postcards of these vessels.

I have tried, within the constraints of publishing, to maintain a chronological integrity and, where possible, introduce ships as they joined the company's fleet, continuing then with the story of that vessel until its end.

The rise and fall of the White Star Line was pretty well mirrored by the popularity of the postcard. Millions of cards were posted daily just prior to the First World War at which time, before the loss of the *Titanic* in 1912, the company had arguably reached a commercial zenith. By the time of White Star's enforced merger with Cunard in 1934, the telephone had begun to replace the postcard as a means of communication.

All the postcards featured within this book come from my own collection. Whenever possible I have acknowledged not only the original artist but also the publisher of each postcard and, where shown, the tonnage is 'gross registered'. Should you, the reader, seek further information on any particular vessel, I can recommend the excellent publications mentioned in the bibliography section of this book.

I hope you enjoy my selection of postcards. They were fascinating to collect!

Patrick Mylon
London 2011

▲ Teutonic (1889–1921).

▲ Majestic I (1890–1914).

▲ Cymric (1898–1916).

▲ Cedric (1903–31).

'Woven in Silk' postcards appear to have been discontinued after the First World War but were popular during the preceding years. Marked on the reverse is 'Inland Postage Only' and *Cedric*'s also has the notation 'This space as well as the back may now be used for communication (Post Office regulation)' on the left-hand side. This reflects the Post Office's decision, in 1902, to allow divided backs on postcards.

ACKNOWLEDGEMENTS

I am indebted to the following for all their contributions to this book:

Caroline Mylon and Iain Yardley provided much assistance, and showed great patience to a technological dinosaur!

Janet Smith for her tireless genealogical research.

Carolyn de la Plain for all her enthusiastic support over many years.

Inger Moss for translating Swedish into English despite being Norwegian!

Those really nice people at The History Press for their excellent design and creativity, and especially Amy Rigg for her encouragement and support and even the choice of the title!

Finally the postcard and memorabilia dealers, auction houses and collectors with whom I have dealt over the last thirty years.

All images from the author's collection unless otherwise stated and every effort has been made to trace copyright holders where appropriate. Should anyone have been inadvertently overlooked, the author offers sincere apologies and asks to be contacted via the publishers.

CHAPTER ONE

EARLY DAYS AND RECORD BREAKERS

SPECIAL.

WHITE STAR LINE.
PASSENGER DEPARTMENT.
——o——
LIVERPOOL, 7th December, 1892.

TO OUR AGENTS.

Please <u>note</u> the following :—
SALOON.
TEUTONIC, 14th Dec.—The £12 Berths are now all let, and with the Saloon accommodation well filled, please secure an allotment of Berths before definitely Booking any more Saloon Passengers.

The BRITANNIC, 21st, and ADRIATIC, 23th instant, have vacant accommodation from £10 10s. upwards.

SECOND CABIN.
TEUTONIC, 14th Dec.—The £7 10s. Berths are filling rapidly, but there is still Ample Room at the £8 10s. rate (in Two-Berth and Four-Berth Outside Rooms.

STEERAGE.
You may book Steerage Passengers for TEUTONIC, 14th December, and later Sailings, on the conditions named in our Circular, dated 2nd instant. Rates £5, MAJESTIC and TEUTONIC ; £4 10s., BRITANNIC, GERMANIC, ADRIATIC and CELTIC.

INLAND BOOKING—You may resume booking Inland as per our Post Card of the 25th ultimo.

When communicating regarding Passengers, do not omit to name the Class, "Saloon, Second Cabin or Steerage, also Sex," and make all remittances payable to

ISMAY, IMRIE & CO.

◄ *Teutonic*'s sailing on 14 December is busy in Saloon and Second Cabin classes, but Steerage less so, according to this 'Fleet Advisory' sent on 7 December 1892 by White Star's Passenger Dept to agent De Vries & Co. in Amsterdam. The information was received on 10 December, allowing little time for booking! The various rates make interesting reading. This practice of mailing fleet and booking information appears not to have been carried into the twentieth century.

BIRD'S EYE VIEW OF TRAFALGAR SQUARE AND ENVIRONS.
OCEANIC HOUSE, 1. COCKSPUR STREET, THE LONDON WEST END OFFICES OF THE WHITE STAR
AND ASSOCIATED LINES WILL BE SEEN IN THE FOREGROUND.

White Star Offices, Liverpool.

▲ Until White Star Line's purchase by the International Mercantile Marine Company (IMMC), the London offices were located in small premises at 17 Cockspur Street near Trafalgar Square. Oceanic House was completed in May 1905 and housed, as well as White Star, the offices of all the IMMC-controlled companies. Oceanic House was designed by architect Henry Tanner Jr and is located at 1 Cockspur Street. Housed in the same building were the London offices of Belfast shipbuilder Harland & Wolff who built the majority of White Star Line vessels. A passenger transit lounge was located on the first floor.

◀ The headquarters building of the White Star Line was located at 30 James Street, Liverpool, and designed by the architect Richard Norman Shaw, who had also designed the London offices of the Metropolitan Police at Scotland Yard. White Star's offices were located here from December 1897 until their purchase by the Royal Mail Group in 1929 when business was transferred to the new owner's head office in Leadenhall Street, London. The building on this card suffered badly from a German bombing raid during the Second World War but has since been restored. This card, by Valentine's, was posted from Liverpool in June 1906.

Not a very busy day at Pier 48 New York! *Teutonic* or *Majestic* preparing for a return passage to Liverpool. The words NEW YORK–WHITE STAR LINE–LIVERPOOL are on the building.

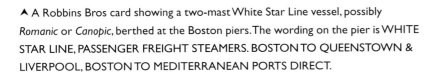

White Star Line, Boston, Mass.

⌃ A Robbins Bros card showing a two-mast White Star Line vessel, possibly *Romanic* or *Canopic*, berthed at the Boston piers. The wording on the pier is WHITE STAR LINE, PASSENGER FREIGHT STEAMERS. BOSTON TO QUEENSTOWN & LIVERPOOL, BOSTON TO MEDITERRANEAN PORTS DIRECT.

⌃ The White Star Line wharf at Millar's Point, Sydney, NSW with a cargo vessel, possibly *Delphic*, moored alongside. The postage stamp was issued by the state of NSW and not Australia.

WHITE STAR LINE.

Royal & United States
WEEKLY

Mail Steamers
ITINERARY.

Liverpool & New York Service.

MAJESTIC—Arr. NEW YORK, 6-0 a.m.. 12th April,
   Passage **5** days **22** hours.
TEUTONIC—Arr. QUEENSTOWN, 10-27 a.m., 12th April.
BRITANNIC—Left QUEENSTOWN, 1-20 p.m. 13th April
GERMANIC—Left NEW YORK, 4-0 p.m., 12th April.
ADRIATIC—In DOCK, LIVERPOOL.

TEUTONIC—Leaves LIVERPOOL, 19th April.
MAJESTIC—Leaves NEW YORK, 19th April.

CARGO STEAMERS.

BOVIC—Left NEW YORK, 8 a.m., 12th April.
NARONIC—Left LIVERPOOL, 6-30 a.m. 11th Feb.
TAURIC—Left LIVERPOOL, 3-0 p.m., 7th April.
NOMADIC—In DOCK, LIVERPOOL.
RUNIC—Arr. NEW YORK, midnight, 11th April.
CUFIC—Left NEW YORK, 8-0 p.m., 4th April.

CUFIC—Leaves LIVERPOOL, 21st April.
RUNIC—Leaves NEW YORK, 18th April.

London & New Zealand Service

DORIC—Left CAPETOWN, 7th April.
IONIC—Left CAPETOWN, 6th April.
COPTIC—Left TENERIFFE, 12th April.

COPTIC—Leaves LONDON, 11th May.
DORIC—Leaves NEW ZEALAND, 13th May.

San Francisco, Japan & China Service.

BELGIC—Left YOKOHAMA, 8th April.
GAELIC—Left SAN FRANCISCO, 4th April.
OCEANIC—Arr. HONG KONG, 7th April.

BELGIC—Leaves SAN FRANCISCO, 4th May.
OCEANIC—Leaves HONG KONG, 18th April.

LIVERPOOL, 13th April, 1893.   ISMAY, IMRIE & CO.

⌃ A Royal & United States Mail Steamers 'Weekly Itinerary' posted to agent Brasch
& Rothenstein in Leipzig, Germany on 13 April 1893. Interestingly the card mentions
Majestic's record crossing as well as the departure of the *Naronic*, which disappeared,
without trace, on that same voyage in February 1893. White Star's short-lived trans-
Pacific service is also included.

S.S. "Britannia," Liverpool   Valentines Series

◀ The 5,004-ton *Britannic* was laid down at Harland & Wolff, Belfast, as *Hellenic* but her name was changed prior to launching in February 1874. She reduced the average transatlantic crossing time by one day and broke the existing speed records in both directions. Although similar to P&O's *Britannia*, this image is clearly White Star's *Britannic* as indicated by the funnel tops and the White Star pennant on the foremast. By the time this Valentine's card was posted from Liverpool on 26 March 1904, the *Britannic* was no more, having been towed to Hamburg for scrapping in July 1903.

➤ Christmas 1903! Another postcard depicting *Britannic* with her name misspelt. Posted on Christmas Eve 1903, this Ludwig Blattner card shows her here as Boer War troopship No.62 with white-painted hull, and as such she made ten return voyages to South Africa. Note the festive glitter on her masts and rigging!

Photo Etching   White Star Liner „S. S. Britanic" copyright

Ludwig Blättner & Co., Produced at the works in Germany

⌃ *Britannic*'s sister-ship *Germanic* at sea with auxiliary sails unfurled.

⌃ The second *Oceanic* at Southampton.

⌃ *Cretic* at Gibraltar, on the USA–Mediterranean service.

Four unpublished White Star Line proofs from paintings by the artist Norman Wilkinson (1878–1971).

⌄ *Laurentic* (I) at Quebec operating the joint White Star-Dominion Line service to Canada.

Liverpool. R. M. S. Germanic. leaving Landing Stage.

R. M. S. Ottawa. (Dominion Line.)

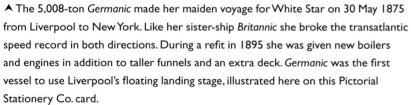

▲ The 5,008-ton *Germanic* made her maiden voyage for White Star on 30 May 1875 from Liverpool to New York. Like her sister-ship *Britannic* she broke the transatlantic speed record in both directions. During a refit in 1895 she was given new boilers and engines in addition to taller funnels and an extra deck. *Germanic* was the first vessel to use Liverpool's floating landing stage, illustrated here on this Pictorial Stationery Co. card.

▲ In 1903 the *Germanic* was transferred within the IMMC, briefly to the American Line then to the Dominion Line, and renamed *Ottawa* in 1905. Not to be thwarted by this change, the same publisher re-issued the postcard reflecting the new funnel colours and name!

AVONMOUTH DOCKS.   HB&S

◄ The *Ottawa* operated the Dominion Line service from Liverpool to Canada (Halifax in winter and Montreal and Quebec in summer) until 1911. Here she is seen at Avonmouth Docks. Note the cross-masts still on her forward mast.

➤ In 1911 *Ottawa* was sold to a Turkish company and renamed *Gul-Djemal* (Rose) as shown on this Nautical Photo Agency card. During the First World War she was sold to the Turkish government as a troopship and, as such, carried troops to the Dardanelles to fight the British and the French! In 1920–21 she operated an emigrant service from Turkey to New York and later operated in the Black Sea. She was renamed *Gulcemal* in 1928, still in government ownership, and after having been used as a store-ship in Istanbul she was towed to Messina for breaking up in 1950. An incredibly long service life of seventy-five years!

Gul-Djémal. "Nautical."   42.

281 — LA PALLICE-ROCHELLE - Le Paquebot "Gaelic"
L. C.

◄ The 4,206-ton *Gaelic* sailed on her maiden voyage from Liverpool to New York before joining the White Star Line's Occidental & Oriental Pacific service where she made her first crossing on 10 November 1885. This postcard, mailed in 1905, shows her as the Pacific Steam Navigation Company's (PSNC) *Callao* despite the name *Gaelic* being indicated. The PSNC purchased and renamed her in 1905 for use on their South American routes until she was scrapped in South Wales in 1907.

► The SS *Persia*, built by Harland & Wolff, Belfast as *Coptic* for White Star Line in 1881. She was originally intended for Occidental & Oriental's Pacific service but, from 1884 to 1894, served the joint White Star – Shaw Savill & Albion (SS & A) New Zealand service. White Star provided vessels and their crews and SS & A handled management. Captain E.J. Smith was on her bridge for her maiden voyage on 16 November 1881, and also between 1889 and 1894. He was later to lose his life as commander of the ill-fated *Titanic* in 1912. In 1906 the *Coptic* was sold to the Pacific Mail S.S. Co. and renamed *Persia*. She was later sold to a Japanese company in 1915, renamed *Persia Maru* and finally broken up in Osaka in 1926.

S. S. Persia - 1913 -

◄ The 4,639-ton *Cufic*, on this Nautical Photo Agency card, and her sister-ship *Runic*, were the last single screw ships to be built for the White Star Line. She sailed on her maiden voyage in December and was, in 1895, also commanded by Captain E.J. Smith. She was constructed to carry livestock (cattle) eastbound and general cargo on the return voyage from Liverpool to New York.

➤ In 1901 the *Cufic* was sold to the Dominion Line and renamed *Manxman*. She served with Elder Dempster Line and the Shipping Controller in the First World War. Sold to the Universal Transport Co. of New York and still named *Manxman*, she was lost in February 1919 with all forty hands whilst en route to Gibraltar from the US, with a cargo of wheat.

R. M. S. TEUTONIC
Paquebot Poste Rapide à double hélices
par grosse mer au large de X...

▲ The 9,984-ton *Teutonic* was launched at Harland & Wolff in 1889 and, with her sister-ship *Majestic*, was the first Belfast-built White Star vessel with twin screws and no sails. With a maximum speed of 20 knots she took the westbound speed record in 1891 and held it for a year. Grimaud, the French publisher of this card, frequently depicted vessels in stormy seas!

H.M.T. TEUTONIC
LEAVING SOUTHAMPTON

∧ Prior to her maiden voyage the *Teutonic* attended the Spithead Royal Naval Review in 1889. She, and her sister *Majestic*, were the first merchant vessels to comply with Admiralty cruiser requirements and at this time the *Teutonic* was armed with eight 4.7-inch guns. The German Kaiser Wilhelm II was also in attendance at this review. The *Teutonic* was taken over for trooping duties during the Boer War and this card was posted in 1902 with the message: *Just a p.c. to let you know we have got to Gib. alright.*

▲ In 1907 *Teutonic* was one of the White Star vessels to switch her home port from Liverpool to Southampton to better attract the European market at Cherbourg. On 16 June 1909 she is seen here having run aground on Sandy Hook on the edge of the Ambrose Channel. Her engines are 'full astern' in an attempt to free herself, which she succeeded in doing after two-and-a-half hours' aground.

◄ The message on this Art Publishing Co. card, posted from Queenstown on 25 September 1909, *Goodbye. Remember me to All,* must have been written by countless millions during the emigrant movement from Europe to the USA and Canada, as people turned their backs on 'The Old World'.

➤ Posted on Christmas Eve 1901, this Hugo Lang & Co. postcard records one of the rare occasions that *Teutonic* and *Majestic* would have been together at Liverpool. This is before *Majestic* had had one of her masts removed during a re-fit in 1902. Note the Christmas carol message: *I saw three ships come sailing in. On Xmas Day in the Morning!*

R. M. S. Majestic and Teutonic.

" I saw three Ships come sailing in !
" On Xmas Day in the Morning!

39424 Published by Hugo Lang & Co., Liverpool.

R. M. S. Majestic.

with larger funnels.

The Wrench Series, No. 3179

◄ The 9,965-ton *Majestic* sailed on her maiden voyage from Liverpool to New York on 2 April 1890. In July 1891 she captured the westbound record with an average speed of 20.1 knots. She lost it to her sister *Teutonic* a month later. The two sisters were the last White Star vessels built for speed and possibly the first to dispense with sails. This Wrench picture of *Majestic* had been taken after her funnels were extended but before her masts were reduced from three to two. Both are said to have taken place during her refit of 1902–03!

White Star Liner "R. M. S. Arabie".   Copyright.

Ludwig Blättner & Co., New Brighton, produced at the works in Saxony.

➤ After her 1902–03 refit, with her tonnage increased to 10,147 and sporting two masts and taller funnels, *Majestic* is shown here by Ludwig Blattner & Co. incorrectly as 'R.M.S. Arabie'! Note the tender *Magnetic* alongside.

S.S. MAJESTIC.

▲ Like her sister *Teutonic*, the *Majestic* was also switched to operate from Southampton in 1907. In 1911 she was laid up in reserve at Birkenhead but, after the loss of the *Titanic* in 1912, she was hurriedly brought back into service to cover the gaps in the timetable vacated by the ill-fated vessel. In this capacity she is seen here at Southampton, from where this card was posted on 6 August 1913.

◄ In May 1914 *Majestic* arrived at Morecambe for demolition as illustrated on this card by Chas. Finey Bare. Prior to her breaking up she was opened to the public for inspection. Had the powers-that-be been aware of the impending war (which began on 4 August) she might well have been spared!

Promenade Central, Morecambe

➤ In this general view of the Central Promenade at Morecambe, the nearly demolished hull of the *Majestic* can be clearly seen on the right-hand side of the photograph. The card was posted from Morecambe on 12 May 1918.

Liners at Liverpool Landing Stage   No. 12.

◄ The 619-ton *Magnetic*, built at Belfast in 1891 to act as a passenger tender to the White Star vessels at Liverpool, would, at peak times, occasionally help with tender duties at Queenstown in Ireland and was also used for towing. She accompanied *Teutonic* to Queen Victoria's Diamond Jubilee Review at Spithead in 1897. *Magnetic* was the first White Star vessel to be converted to oil burning in the early twenties and is seen here in the Mersey with, probably, *Regina* in the left background.

➤ In 1932 the *Magnetic* was sold to the Alexandra Towing Co. of Liverpool and renamed *Ryde*, depicted here by B & A Feilden. Two years later she became an excursion vessel based at Llandudno and was finally scrapped at Port Glasgow in 1935.

S.T. RYDE.

◄ The 5,728-ton *Tauric* and her sister-ship, *Nomadic*, were built at Harland & Wolff as cattle carriers for the White Star Line and joined the fleet in 1891. Twin-screw vessels, they were employed on the Liverpool to New York service. Both vessels were switched, within the IMMC, to the Dominion Line in 1903.

▼ After her transfer to the Dominion Line, *Tauric* was renamed *Welshman* in 1904 and is seen here at the Royal Edward Dock at Avonmouth. Having been transferred to Frederick Leyland & Co., remaining in Dominion colours, in 1921, she was scrapped at the Firth of Forth in 1929.

➤ The *Nomadic* was also transferred to the Dominion Line in 1903, but not before she achieved the distinction of being the first White Star vessel to be used as a horse carrier, as HMT No. 34, during the Boer War in 1899. She was renamed *Cornishman* in 1904 and is seen here at Portland, Maine on this Berry Paper Co. card. The message, probably from a member of the crew, mailed from Portland on 20 July 1908 reads: *This is the steamer I came over on, had a good passage and wasn't sick. Cornishman* was transferred to Leyland Line in 1921 and broken up in Cornwall in 1926.

S.S. Gothic on fire Plymouth Sound June 4·06

▲ After serving the Shipping Controller under the Liner Requisition Scheme from 1917 to 1919, the *Bovic* returned to the White Star Line but was transferred to the Leyland Line in 1922 and renamed *Colonian*. We see her here after her masts had been restored to their normal height. She was scrapped at Rotterdam in 1928.

◄ The 6,583-ton *Bovic* was built, like her sister-ship *Naronic*, in 1892 as a livestock carrier with limited passenger accommodation. In February 1893 *Naronic* disappeared en route to New York from Liverpool with seventy-four persons on board. Two of her lifeboats, one overturned, were sighted but neither yielded any further information and her fate remains a mystery. In 1914 *Bovic* was transferred to the joint White Star-Leyland-Lamport & Holt service from Manchester to New York and is seen here at Salford Docks with her masts cut down to facilitate her passage under the bridges of the Manchester Ship Canal. The message *This is a view of one of the boats we work on and some of them is larger than this one* could be from either a crew member or dock-worker.

▲ The 7,755-ton *Gothic* was launched at Harland & Wolff, Belfast in 1892 and joined the White Star Line in 1893, operating the joint route to Australasia with SS & A. The twin-screw vessel was built to accommodate 104 first- and 114 third-class passengers as well as refrigerated cargo. On 7 June 1906 her cargo of wool caught fire and she was beached near Plymouth Sound. The salvaged and repaired *Gothic* rejoined the White Star fleet eight months later.

"Gothland".

▲ In 1907 the *Gothic* was transferred to the Red Star Line and renamed *Gothland* but rejoined White Star in 1911, again as *Gothic*, and was refitted to accommodate 1,500 steerage passengers to Australia. Two years later she reverted back to Red Star as *Gothland*. In June of 1914 she ran aground off the Scilly Isles and we see her here, on this Gibsons card, with empty lifeboat falls and one of her boats under tow.

▲ A further view of the stranded *Gothland*. All her 281 passengers were taken off and she remained aground for three days. After refloating, repairs at Southampton took six months. She was scrapped at the Firth of Forth in 1926.

▲ The 8,301-ton *Cevic* was built in 1894 to replace the lost *Naronic*. She was the last of White Star's cattle boats and, initially employed on the Atlantic from Liverpool to New York, was switched to the Australian route via the Cape in 1908.

◄ In 1914, after the outbreak of the First World War, *Cevic* returned to Harland & Wolff and was converted into the 'dummy' battlecruiser HMS *Queen Mary* and is seen here in that disguise. Her guns were made of wood but she was armed with one three-pounder gun and her conversion took from 1 December 1914 to 11 February 1915.
In September 1915 she was restored to her original design and after three name changes, and as many owners, she was finally towed to Genoa and broken up in 1933. The real HMS *Queen Mary* blew up at the Battle of Jutland in 1916.

◄ At 10,077 tons the *Georgic* was, in 1895, the largest livestock carrier ever built. She was, like the majority of White Star's vessels, built at Harland & Wolff in Belfast and remained on the US East Coast service from Liverpool for her entire career. At the outbreak of the First World War she continued to operate her commercial route but, on 10 December 1916, she was apprehended by the German commerce raider *Moewe* whilst en route to Liverpool from Philadelphia. Her crew having been taken off, the *Georgic* was shelled and sunk with her cargo of 10,000 barrels of oil and, very sadly, 1,200 horses. She was the largest vessel to be sunk by the *Moewe*.

▼ The twin-screw *Delphic* was launched at Harland & Wolff and joined White Star in 1897. The 8,273-ton vessel was designed to carry up to 1,000 immigrants and cargo and to operate on the joint service to New Zealand with SS & A via the Cape. During the Boer War, in 1900, she served as a troop transport on the UK–Cape section of her voyage. In 1917 she was taken over by the UK Government under the Liner Requisition Scheme and, on 17 August of that year, she was torpedoed and sunk by UC-72, with the loss of five lives, whilst en route to Montevideo with a cargo of coal. This W. Ferrier postcard was addressed to Mrs Mary Ogilvie, whose address is given as just 'Suva' and was posted from New Zealand in 1914.

THE DELPHIC AND THE SUFFOLK AT THE MAIN WHARF TIMARU. N.Z.   W. FERRIER.

"HANDS ACROSS THE SEA."

S. S. Cymric
(Twin Screw) 13096 Tons.
Length 585 ½ ft. Breadth 64 ⅓ ft.

⋏ Initially planned as a large cattle and cargo carrier, the 13,096-ton *Cymric* joined White Star's fleet in 1898 designed to carry 258 first- and 1,160 third-class passengers on the New York run from Liverpool. She was one of the first vessels to reflect the company's 'size over speed' policy and proved to be very popular and profitable. During the Boer War she made two return voyages to the Cape, as HMT No.74, in 1900. In 1903 she switched from New York to Boston for the next ten years and, in 1913, was altered to carry second- and third-class passengers only. On 8 May 1916 she was torpedoed and sunk off Fastnet by U20 under Commander Schwieger, with the loss of five lives. Almost exactly a year previously Schwieger, in U20, had torpedoed and sunk the Cunard liner *Lusitania* with the loss of 1,201 lives. Issued under the popular 'Hands Across the Sea' banner, this 'British Series' card carried a poem printed on the reverse:

Love is a Question

When thoughts of my troubled mind is past and gone,
Shall happy thoughts succeed.
I am told to ease my troubled mind,
Sleep is a friend you need;
With my pen I penned these lines
You will in them a question find.
My question's grand, so find it if you can
Love is acceptor when in doubt

The author is anonymous!

CHAPTER TWO

EMIGRATION AND EXPANSION

▲ The 11,948-ton *Afric* was, with her sister-ships *Medic* and *Persic*, built to provide a monthly passenger (320 third class) and cargo service on the fast-growing route to Australia. Despite being the first of the trio to be built, she went back to Harland & Wolff for a seven-month improvement refit, thus her sister *Medic* was to inaugurate the service. Completed in 1899, from 1900 to 1902 the *Afric* carried troops and horses for the Boer War as HMT No.A19, on the UK to Cape sections of her voyages, and was, in 1915, requisitioned by the Australian government, also as a troopship. This C.W. Hunt card was posted on 4 November 1915 to Devon and the message, written on 17 October, reads: *My Dear Sister, Brother & Dad. Just a line to say I am keeping in good health and have had a splendid voyage so far, the weather is getting hotter every day. This is the ship we are sailing in very steady. Well my friends I hope this will find you all much better so goodbye and God bless you from your loving Brother Sid xxx.* Above the message Sid has written 'On Active Service' and there is a government stamp which states 'H.M. SHIP. NO CHARGE TO BE RAISED'. The *Afric* was torpedoed and sunk in February 1917 by UC-66 in the English Channel, en route from Liverpool to Sydney, with the loss of twenty-two lives.

◄ *Medic* operated the first White Star sailing to Australia on 3 August 1899 departing Liverpool for Sydney via the Cape. During the Boer War, like her sister *Afric*, she carried troops to South Africa. This card, another by C.W. Hunt, was posted on board and the message reads: *We are nearing the Cape hope to get in on Wed. We have had sports and fancy dress. S.S.Medic Oct. 9/1911.* After serving under the Government's Liner Requisition Scheme from 1917 to 1919, *Medic* was sold in 1928, converted into a whale factory ship, renamed *Hektoria*, and her 11,985 tonnage was increased to 13,834. She was torpedoed and sunk in 1942 in the North Atlantic, as an oil tanker, by U608, having previously been damaged by a torpedo from U211.

➤ The *Persic* was completed within ten weeks of her launch in 1899. This H.W. Flatt card, posted on board at Cape Town, carries the message: *We one and all wish you all a very Merry Xmas and Happy New Year. We have had some terrible weather – were very seasick. They have just sighted the Runic. We have stowaways on board – they are going to be put off.*

White Star Liner, S. S. PERSIC.

▲ *Persic* again on another card by C.W. Hunt. Sent by a member of the Australian Expeditionary Force at Aden on 13 March 1916, the message reads: *Having a fine time. I am enjoying myself greatly. What do you think of the boat?* The words '*On Active Service*' have been written above. Having served under the Liner Requisition Scheme with her sister *Medic*, the *Persic* was refitted by Harland & Wolff at Govan in 1920, laid up in the Mersey in 1926 and finally dismantled in the Netherlands in July 1927.

▲ The 12,482-ton *Runic* and her sister *Suevic* were slightly larger than the preceding three vessels in that they had a continuous bridge and poop deck instead of an island superstructure. The twin-screw vessel was launched at Harland & Wolff in 1900 and departed on her maiden voyage from Liverpool to Sydney on 19 January 1901, with passenger accommodation for 420 in third class and a refrigerated compartment with a capacity for 100,000 carcasses of mutton. After war service from 1917 to 1919 she was refitted at Harland & Wolff in 1921. The message on this 'Star Photo' card reads: *I hear that we can post letters in Plymouth so this will serve to tell of our arrival. We should land in London the day you get this. Had quite a good voyage so far. Sister wants to return on this boat in November.* In 1930 the *Runic* was sold, converted into a whaling ship and renamed *New Sevilla*. She was torpedoed and sunk, whilst in convoy, on 20 October 1940 off Galway with the loss of two lives.

∧ *Suevic* was the last of the five vessels built for the service to Australia and joined the White Star Line in 1901. On 17 March 1907 she ran aground in fog near the Lizard, at full speed, due to a navigational miscalculation. This postcard of the stranded vessel was posted at Penzance on 20 April 1907 and the message reads: *Dear Pattie – am sending you the p.c. of the 'Suevic' that went ashore off the Lizard a few weeks ago.*

▲ The 382 passengers were taken off the stranded *Suevic* using the ship's own lifeboats as well as two shore-based lifeboats. After investigation, it was decided to free
the largely undamaged section, from the bridge aft, by dynamiting that portion away
from the firmly grounded bow. Printed on the front of this E.A. Bragg card are the
words 'Salvage operations on the White Star Liner "Suevic" the XX indicates where
she is being cut in two. The AA portion will be left on the rocks'.

WRECK OF THE WHITE STAR LINER "SUEVIC" Nº 9
SALVAGE FEAT. THIS PHOTOGRAPH SHOWS THE LARGE LINER CUT IN TWO. THE STERN PORTION BEING TOWED TO SOUTHAMPTON THE BOW PORTION REMAINING ON THE LIZARD ROCKS.

⋏ Another postcard by the same publisher and we see the two halves of the *Suevic* after the successful separation. The printing on the front of the card reads: 'Wreck of the White Star liner "Suevic"--- salvage feat. This photograph shows the large liner cut in two, the stern portion being towed to Southampton, the bow portion remaining on the Lizard rocks.'

WRECK OF THE "SUEVIC" SHOWING THE BOW PORTION (ABOUT 184 F.) WHICH IS LEFT ON THE ROCK AT THE LIZARD.

⋀ The abandoned bow of the *Suevic* was left to the ravages of the sea as shown on another E.A. Bragg card posted at Plymouth on 4 July 1907. The message reads: *There is still a bit of the 'Suevic' to be seen on the rocks at the Lizard, but only at low tide. I saw the piece on Monday. Arthur.* The bow was destroyed in a storm during the night of 9/10 May.

◄ The salvaged section of the *Suevic* arrives in Southampton using her own engines in reverse. The four tugs, on this G.D. Courtney card, are assisting with steering.

➤ Successfully moored at Southampton on this card by Frith. The *Suevic*'s salvaged cargo was insured but the cost of the vessel was covered by the White Star Line.

S.S. "SUEVIC"
in Trafalgar. Dock

▲ The stern section of *Suevic*, with undamaged engines, boilers and passenger accommodation, was finally moved to Southampton's Trafalgar Dock to await a new forward section.

Yours old friend in Belfast Millicent 23. 10. '07.

Launch of Bow of S.S. Suevic from Messrs. Harland & Wolff's, Belfast, 5th Oct., 1907.

◄ On the first of two postcards by J.W. Boyd we see the launch of *Suevic*'s newly constructed bow section. Posted on 23 October 1907 to France, the message reads: *My Dear Friend. Here I am again in Belfast with my sister for the day. These cards, although of a very poor kind, I thought would be of interest to you as…* (continued on second card). The sender has written on the front of the card *Your old friend in Belfast. Millicent.*

➤ The message continued …*they are rather unique. You may remember reading in the paper that the White Star liner Suevic went ashore on the 17th March last at the Lizard. She was cut in two and they have made this new bow in Belfast and it has been taken over to Southampton there to be joined.* Written on the front, this time, is the message *A hearty handshake. Millicent 23.10.07.*

A hearty handshake Millicent 23. 10 . '07.

After the Launch of Bow of S.S. Suevic from Queen's Island, Belfast, 5th Oct., 1907.

TOWING NEW BOW OF S.S. "SUEVIC," BELFAST TO SOUTHAMPTON.

PHOTO BY BAIRD, BELFAST.

◄ The departure of *Suevic*'s new 212ft bow from Belfast being towed by a paddle steamer with the tug for steering assistance. This Baird postcard was sent from Belfast on 6 December 1907.

➤ *Suevic*'s new bow safely moored at Southampton on 27 October 1907. Her name and port of registry are clearly visible on the 'stern'. The photograph is the work of local photographer Herbert Willsteed, who published his photos as postcards and sold them to local outlets.

WILLSTEED

S. S. SUEVICS' NEW BOW SOUTHAMPTON, OCT 27TH 1907. 3.

S.S. "SUEVIC" IN DRY DOCK, SOUTHAMPTON

▲ F.G.O. Stuart's close-up of *Suevic*'s stern section clearly showing the effects of the dynamite used to free her from the Lizard. Note the size of the five men standing in the Trafalgar Dock.

POSITIVELY NO ENTRANCE

S/C

NEW PART.
JOINING UP THE "SUEVIC" IN THE TRAFALGAR DOCK

◄ A postcard sent from Southampton to Cheshire by one of the men working on the repairs to *Suevic*. The message reads: *My squad has been here for nearly 4 weeks and the Suevic will last another week yet. We hope other work will come in to keep us going for a little longer. Joe.* Work began joining the two parts on 26 October 1907 and *Suevic* resumed service in January 1908. The photograph shows the old and new sections with a dotted line indicating the join.

▲ In 1915 the *Suevic* made one trooping voyage to the Dardanelles in addition to her normal service but was requisitioned in 1917 for trooping duties as HMT No. A29. After the war she was refitted and resumed her Australian service. She was sold in 1928, converted into a whaling ship and renamed *Skytteren*. On 1 April 1942 she was scuttled off Sweden, to escape capture by German armed trawlers.

Two further illustrations by artist Norman Wilkinson featured on unpublished White Star Line proofs.

◄ *Runic* at Cape Town.

➤ *Suevic* at Sydney.

S.S. Irishman

◄ The 9,540-ton *Irishman* was built at Harland & Wolff in 1899 for the North Atlantic cattle and general service of the Dominion Line but, at some time, must have been transferred within the IMMC to White Star as indicated by this C.W. Hunt card. The message on this card, posted at Cape Town to the UK on 21 October 1910, reads: *Dere Persie. I am doing as well as possible time goes slow it will take nine weeks to go but it will soon pass over from your loving brother Arnie.* Punctuation was, it seems, of little importance!

➤ A Valentine's postcard of an 'Afric' class liner has been over-printed top left 'S.S. Irishman'. This was a frequent occurrence as, within the IMMC, several vessels were switched between companies. It had not been considered worthwhile to produce postcards this time unless maybe they had sold out! Posted at Liverpool on 21 March 1914, the message reads: *Dear Em. Just on board alright. Love Jim.* The *Irishman* was transferred to the Leyland Line in 1921 and broken up in Germany in 1926.

S. S. IRISHMAN.

▼ The *Oceanic* was the first vessel to exceed the length of Brunel's *Great Eastern* and was ordered by White Star from Harland & Wolff to compete with North German Lloyd's *Kaiser Wilhelm der Grosse* and Cunard's *Campania* and *Lucania*. Over 50,000 people attended her launching in January 1899 and, at the time of her completion in September, she was the largest and most luxurious vessel afloat. This Express Photographic Co. card clearly shows off her enormous funnels and the flying boat makes an interesting appearance.

S. S. Oceanic
*sailing
from Liverpool*

The Wrench Series,
No. 2709

◄ The 17,274-ton *Oceanic* departing Liverpool, in this painting by William Wyllie, on a Wrench card. Initially there was bad vibration at her stern whilst at full speed. A sister-ship, *Olympic*, was ordered but abandoned in 1899 after the death of Thomas Ismay. He had not been well enough to travel on *Oceanic*'s maiden voyage.

➤ *Oceanic* was one of the first White Star vessels to be constructed under the new 'size and comfort' policy, which resulted in a considerable reduction in coal consumption. The first-class dining saloon was placed between her giant funnels. This White Star-produced card of *Oceanic*'s library illustrates the elegance of the vessel.

R. M. S. OCEANIC, LIBRARY

⋀ The *Oceanic* was one of four White Star Line vessels to inaugurate the company's express service from Southampton in 1907. In 1912, after a coal-miners' strike, she surrendered her coal to enable *Titanic* to sail on her maiden voyage. At the outbreak of the First World War she was taken over by the Admiralty, converted into an armed merchant cruiser with sixteen 4.7in guns and allocated to the Tenth Cruiser Squadron. Sadly, however, on 8 September 1914, she was wrecked twenty miles west of Shetland in calm weather, whilst under the command of a RN officer inexperienced in handling large passenger liners. In 1924 the wreck was broken up in situ and the final removal of the vessel took place between 1973 and 1979. This image of *Oceanic*, by artist Charles Padday on a White Star Line proof, slightly exaggerates her funnel height.

∧ Four colourful postcards featuring images of White Star Line vessels framed by national flags. (*Cymric* by Valentine's, *Celtic* by C.W. Hunt & Co.)

S. S. CELTIC.

▲ Celtic was the last vessel to be ordered from Harland & Wolff by Thomas Ismay, White Star Line's founder, and the first to exceed 20,000 tons. It is believed that she was an improved version of Oceanic's cancelled sister-ship Olympic. She was the first of a very successful class of liners that came to be known as 'The Big Four'. This promotional card was issued by the White Star Line to mark the launch of Celtic on 4 April 1901.

SOME STATISTICS OF THE
Leviathan Steamship "Celtic,"
LAUNCHED FROM THE YARDS OF
Messrs. Harland & Wolff, Belfast,
4th APRIL, 1901.

Length,	. . . . 700 Feet.	Accommodation for 1st Class, .	. 347
Breadth,	. . . . 75 "	" " 2nd "	. . . 160
Depth,	. . . . 49 "	" " 3rd "	. . 2,352
Gross Register,	. . . . 20,904 Tons.	Crew, ...	. . 335
Net "	. . . . 13,449 "	No. of Decks, ...	. 9
	Displacement at load draft,	. . . 37,700 Tons.	

WHITE STAR LINE,
9 Broadway, New York.

ISMAY, IMRIE & CO.,
Liverpool and London.

TABER
BAS-RELIEF Co.

S.S. CELTIC
LENGTH, 700 FT. BREADTH, 75 FT. TONNAGE, 20,900.

692

◀ *Celtic at sea on a Taber Bas-Relief card. This type of card with a raised profile was popular prior to the First World War. The message on this card, posted from New York to the UK on 23 November 1909, reads: Dear Aunt Mary. I have enclosed you a picture of the ship that carried your boy to America the second time. She was a very fine ship and I enjoyed the trip very much more than I did when I crossed in a sailship in 1883 and was almost eight weeks on the ocean. Harry.*

➤ The White Star Line, eager to promote their vessels, allowed the publisher to produce this card showing *Celtic's* huge size in dry-dock and uncluttered boat deck. The message, having been written on the front of this Wrench card, indicates that this was probably before the Post Office allowed divided backs on postcards in 1902. *Can you see the man standing near one of the screws in the left-hand picture. The depth of the boat as you see it is about 60ft. Love from Reggie.*

➤ A third-class menu for 16 September 1909 on board the *Celtic*. Note that all the meals for the day, in third class, are displayed on one card and 'lunch' becomes 'dinner'. 'Gruel' for supper is a thin porridge. On the reverse of these menus were details of White Star vessels. The, as yet unnamed, *Olympic* and *Titanic* are mentioned as 'Largest Steamers in the World (Bldg.)'.

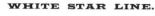

WHITE STAR LINE.

S.S CELTIC AT SEA   SEPTEMBER 16TH 1909
THIRD CLASS.
BREAKFAST
OATMEAL PORRIDGE & MILK
CALVES' LIVER AND BACON   IRISH STEW
FRESH BREAD & BUTTER
SWEDISH BREAD   MARMALADE
TEA   COFFEE
DINNER
VEGETABLE SOUP
ROAST MUTTON AND ONION SAUCE
GREEN PEAS   BAKED & BOILED POTATOES
CABIN BISCUITS   FRESH BREAD
PLUM PUDDING SWEET SAUCE
ORANGES
TEA
BAKED PORK & BEANS
STEWED APRICOTS & RICE   SWEDISH BREAD
FRESH BREAD AND BUTTER
TEA
SUPPER.
CHEESE   CABIN BISCUITS   GRUEL   COFFEE

Any complaint respecting the Food supplied, want of attention or incivility, should be at once reported to the Purser or Chief Steward. For purposes of identification, each Steward wears a numbered badge on the arm.

➤ Second-class menus were printed for each meal and contained more colour than their third-class fellows but were also issued as postcards. White Star encouraged their passengers to mail these cards, thus benefiting from the free advertising. This practice did not extend to first class! This menu for dinner on board the *Majestic* on 3 October 1911 now names, on the reverse, 'Largest and Finest steamers in the World – *Olympic & Titanic*', as *Olympic* was now in service.

WHITE STAR LINE
TWIN SCREW STEAMER "MAJESTIC."
2ND. CLASS.
DINNER.
OCT 3RD 1911
CONSOMME FLEURY
BOILED HALIBUT, HOLLANDAISE SAUCE
SWEETBREAD CROQUETTES, PERIGORDINE
BOILED FOWL & BACON, PARSLEY SAUCE
SIRLOIN OF BEEF WITH GREEN PEPPERS
PARSNIPS A LA CREME   HARICOT BEANS
BOILED & BROWNED POTATOES
COLLEGE PUDDING
MARBLE JELLY
ICE CREAM
ORANGES   PINEAPPLE   BANANAS   ASSORTED NUTS
CHEESE   BISCUITS
COFFEE

WHITE STAR - DOMINION CANADIAN SERVICE.

TWIN SCREW STEAMER "MEGANTIC."

2ND. CLASS

17TH MAY, 1912

LUNCHEON

CONSOMME SPRING   CLAM CHOWDER

BROILED FILLETS OF WEAKFISH

SEA PIE

CORNED BEEF & VEGETABLES

BAKED JACKET POTATOES

COLD

ROAST BEEF   VEAL & HAM PIE
HOME-MADE BRAWN   ROAST PORK

LETTUCE   RADISHES

SAGO PUDDING   PASTRY

BISCUITS   CHEESE

TEA   COFFEE

⬑ This second-class luncheon menu from the *Megantic* is dated 17 May 1912 and still refers to *Olympic* and *Titanic* on the reverse. *Titanic* had been at the bottom of the Atlantic for over a month by this time!

TWIN SCREW STEAMER "BALTIC."

2ND. CLASS

DINNER   SUNDAY, NOVEMBER 10TH 1912.

HORS DŒUVRES VARIES

CREAM OF TOMATO

FRIED GURNET, PARSLEY SAUCE

SAUTE OF CHICKEN—MARENGO

HAUNCH OF LAMB—MINT SAUCE

ROAST RIBS & SIRLOIN OF BEEF, RAIFORT

POMMES ANGLAISE

BRUSSELS SPROUTS   BOILED RICE

SALADE DE SAISON

COBURG PUDDING   SCOTCH CHEESE CAKES

WINE JELLY

ICE CREAM

ORANGES   PEACHES   PEARS

DESSERT   COFFEE

△ *Baltic*'s second-class dinner menu for 10 November 1912 sent from the ship, postmarked 'Transatlantic Post Office' on 16 November 1912, to the UK with the message: *We expect to reach New York tonight but I don't think we can land until tomorrow (Sat.). I feel rather lonely at times. There are some fine fellows on board. Concert last night. The orchestra plays twice daily. Am quite well – feeling very fit. Have made lots of friends. Cheer up.* By this time only *Olympic* was referred to on the reverse.

TWIN SCREW STEAMER "CORINTHIC."

2ND CLASS

May 30th, 1914

BREAKFAST

Quaker Oats

Kippered Herrings

Split Country Sausage

Hashed Lamb, Creole

Grilled Wiltshire Bacon

Mashed Potatoes

Vienna and Graham Rolls   Sally Lunns

Griddle Cakes, Maple Syrup

Conserve   Marmalade

Tea   Coffee

Watercress

◄ Breakfast on the *Corinthic* in second class on 30 May 1914 would be adequate for any size appetite on this New Zealand service vessel.

WHITE STAR LINE.

JULY 1ST, 1914

R.M.S. "ADRIATIC" THIRD CLASS

BREAKFAST

QUAKER OATS & MILK
FRESH FISH   LIVER AND BACON
TEA   COFFEE   MARMALADE
SWEDISH, KOSHER AND FRESH BREAD

DINNER

BOUILLI SOUP
MINCED TRIPE AND TOMATOES
ROAST PORK, SAGE DRESSING
PUREE OF CARROTS AND TURNIPS
BROWNED AND BOILED POTATOES
RICE PUDDING
FRESH BREAD   CABIN BISCUITS

TEA

COTTAGE PIE   COLD ROAST MUTTON & PICKLES
POTATO SALAD
CURRANT BUNS
CONSERVE   TEA   FRESH, KOSHER & SWEDISH BREAD

SUPPER

GRUEL   BISCUITS   CHEESE   COFFEE

Any complaint respecting the Food supplied, want of attention or incivility, should be at once reported to the Purser or Chief Steward. For purposes of identification each Steward wears a numbered badge.

◄ One month before the outbreak of the First World War, this third-class menu on *Adriatic*, the last of the 'Big Four', features on the reverse the advertisement for 'Triple screw *Britannic* 50,000 tons (launched) and RMS *Olympic*… One of the largest steamers in the world.' How popular might 'Minced Tripe and Tomatoes' be today?

WHITE STAR LINE R.M.S. CELTIC, 21,179 TONS
TOURIST THIRD CABIN DINING SALOON

◄ Following the collapse of emigrant traffic to the USA, the decision was made to refit and reclassify the passenger accommodation on *Celtic* and her sisters. Tourist Third Cabin would be the new name for third class, the better parts of which had been merged with second class to form Tourist Class. We see here the Tourist Third Cabin dining saloon with tables already laid.

➤ This view of the Tourist Third Cabin lounge prepared for dancing was mailed as a postcard on 29 August 1927 with the message: *Thank you for your Bon Voyage cards. We were all glad to have them. We miss all of you and the nice dances. Here is a picture of where we would dance on the ship if you were here. They have good music too.*

WHITE STAR LINE R.M.S. CELTIC, 21,179 TONS
TOURIST THIRD CABIN LOUNGE PREPARED FOR DANCING

▼ On 10 December 1928 the *Celtic* ran aground in a gale near Roches Point at the entrance to Cobh Harbour. Despite all efforts, she could not be freed and it was decided to break her up in situ. Her cargo was unloaded and a Danish company began work on her demolition.

➤ Very shortly after going aground it became necessary to cut *Celtic*'s funnels to deck level as they obstructed the beam of light from the Roches Point lighthouse. The dismantling of *Celtic* was complete by 1933.

HANDS ACROSS THE SEA.

WOVEN IN SILK

R.M.S. CEDRIC.

◄ A 'silk' postcard, featuring the flags of Sweden and the USA with 'crossed hands', mailed from the *Cedric*, second of the 'Big Four', on 17 December 1910 with the message: *On board the steamer Cedric. Everything OK. No rough weather whatever. It is like summer out here on the ocean. Will be in England tomorrow. A Merry Xmas and a happy new year to you all from Carl.* Posted at Liverpool on 19 December to the USA despite card being marked 'Inland Postage Only'!

➤ Another 'silk' card featuring the *Baltic*, third vessel of the 'Big Four', framed by the flags of Britain and the USA.

HANDS ACROSS THE SEA.

WOVEN IN SILK

R.M.S. BALTIC.

▲ A magnificent view of *Athenic* at Wellington, NZ by artist Norman Wilkinson featured on a White Star Line 'proof' card. The *Athenic* was the first of three vessels employed by the company on the joint Shaw Savill and Albion service to New Zealand. White Star provided their ships and crews, which were managed by SSA. The 12,234-ton *Athenic*, built by Harland & Wolff, sailed on her maiden voyage to Wellington in February 1902.

WELLINGTON HARBOUR DURING THE STRIKE. A2875.

▲ On 22 October 1913 the dockers at Wellington went on strike and they were 'locked out' the next day. Six days later 1,000 held a protest meeting which resulted in Special Constables being sent in the next day and, on 8 November Special Constables also occupied the wharves at Auckland leading to a General Strike in New Zealand. The Wellington waterfront strike was called off on 20 December. On this Aldersly card we see here *Athenic*, on the left in Wellington Harbour, stranded by the strike. Behind her is one of her sister-ships, either *Corinthic* or *Ionic*.

◄ During the First World War *Athenic* was employed, under the Liner Requisition Scheme from 1917 to 1919, on trooping duties between the UK and Australasia via the Pacific. She is seen here, in dazzle paint, having run aground on a coral reef in the West Indies on 5 May 1918.

▼ In 1928 *Athenic* was sold to a Norwegian company, converted into a whaling factory ship and renamed *Pelagos*. Captured by the German commerce raider *Pinguin* in 1941, she became a submarine depot ship to Germany's U-boat fleet based in Norway. After the war she resumed her career and was finally broken up in Hamburg in 1962.

Latarche's Library, Publishers 63 Lime St.

R. M. S. Cedric.

HVITA STJERNLINIEN, S.S."CEDRIC"

MODELLEN UTSTÄLLD
I MASKINHALLEN.

▲ *Cedric* was the second of the 'Big Four' liners to be employed on the service from Liverpool to New York. Strangely she is featured here on a Latarche postcard with the French flag. It was, however, her later sister-ship *Adriatic* that operated to the USA via Cherbourg. Posted at Liverpool on 4 December 1908 with a half-penny stamp, the recipient would have had to have paid an additional half-penny as these 'relief' cards were subject to a 'letter rate' of one penny.

➤ A dramatic night view of *Cedric* on a postcard, issued in 1907 by a White Star agent in Sweden, announcing the safe arrival of the *Adriatic* in New York on 4 September having left Southampton on 28 August.

➤ *Cedric* is featured here on a postcard overprinted with New Year greetings for 1906 from Richard B. Green & Co. Ltd. On the reverse is an advertisement for their 'Parsley Brand Salmon'.

CAPETOWN.

GREETINGS SINCERE

1909-10.

R. M. S. CORINTHIC.

WISHING YOU A HAPPY CHRISTMAS
AND A
BRIGHT AND PROSPEROUS NEW YEAR

From Lily & Will

Gould & Son, Harmer St., Gravesend.

◄ *Corinthic*, the second of the New Zealand joint service vessels, illustrated on this Gould card mailed from Cape Town, with an overprinted New Year and Christmas greeting for 1909–10. The 12,231-ton *Corinthic* departed on her maiden voyage to Wellington on 20 November 1902 and, like her sisters, had capacity for 121 first-, 117 second- and 450 third-class passengers.

➤ *Corinthic* served from 1917 to 1919 under the Liner Requisition Scheme, carrying troops in her third-class accommodation, but continued her refrigerated meat service from New Zealand. She is seen here in dazzle-paint camouflage during the latter stage of her war career. Resuming her normal service in 1920 she was, in 1929, converted to 'Cabin' and third class only with the removal of first class and was scrapped at Wallsend in 1931.

▼ *Ionic*, the third vessel of the New Zealand trio, on a postcard issued as a souvenir of the children's party held on board on 9 July 1926. The *Ionic* was, in 1909, the first vessel to New Zealand to carry radio! The set was designed by her second officer but could only receive messages. *Ionic* was transferred to SSA ownership after White Star's merger with Cunard in 1934 and broken up in Japan in 1937. Her ship's bell is still to be seen at Auckland's war museum.

R.M.S. "IONIC"
Souvenir of the
Children's Fancy Dress Parade
and
Tea Party
Held on board, Friday, July, 9th, 1926.

CHAPTER THREE

J. PIERPONT MORGAN

⌃ With the acquisition in 1902 of White Star Line by the International Mercantile Marine Company of American millionaire J. Pierpont Morgan, there followed a re-shuffle of vessels between the various companies within the giant combine. The 8,806-ton *Canada* had been built at Harland & Wolff for the Dominion Line Canadian service in 1896 and was transferred to the White Star-Dominion Line joint service to Canada in 1903. Despite the card shown it is unlikely that she was owned and operated solely by the White Star Line or that her funnel was painted in White Star Line colours.

⌃ An identical image but, this time, *Canada* is depicted in Dominion Line colours. As well as Boer War trooping, as No.69 in 1899, *Canada* was employed as a troopship during the First World War. After her refit in 1919 she emerged 600 tons heavier and as a one class (Cabin) vessel. She continued on the joint service to Canada until being scrapped in Italy in 1926.

S. S. New England.

▼ The 11,394-ton *New England*, on this Pictorial Stationery card, was launched at Harland & Wolff in 1898 for the Dominion Line service from Liverpool to Boston.

S. S. "ROMANIC."

Allan Liner S. S. "Scandinavian".

▲ Despite White Star taking over Dominion Line's profitable Liverpool–Boston route the *New England* was switched to White Star's Boston–Mediterranean service in 1903. Renamed *Romanic*, she was probably the first White Star vessel to sport two masts instead of the usual four. The message on this Hugo Lang card posted to Canada reads: *In sight of land Azores Islands. We go on land for an hour. Love to all.*

▲ *Romanic* was purchased by the Allen Line in 1912 for their Glasgow–Halifax–Boston service and renamed *Scandinavian*. She was taken over in 1915 by Canadian Pacific and served under the Liner Requisition Scheme from 1917 to 1919. After the war she operated from Antwerp to Montreal and was scrapped in Germany in 1923.

Another Dominion Line vessel to be switched to White Star Line was the 15,378-ton *Columbus*. After her transfer in 1903 she was renamed *Republic* and placed in the New York–Mediterranean winter service. In the early hours of 23 January 1909, in thick fog off Nantucket, she was in collision with the Italian emigrant vessel *Florida*. Her passengers, and the majority of her crew, were transferred to the *Florida* and were then later transferred, with *Florida*'s passengers, to White Star's *Baltic*, which had arrived on the scene having answered *Republic*'s distress call. This was probably the first time radio had been used at sea to transmit a distress message. Attempts were made to take *Republic* in tow but she sank at around 8p.m. on 24 January. Four lives were lost in the incident.

➤ The *Florida* berthed at New York after the collision clearly showing, on this Trenkler card, her crumpled bow. White Star successfully sued her owners, Lloyd Italiano, and *Florida* was sold for £40,000 to contribute to the cost.

R. M. S. Commonwealth.

S. S. Canopic

Ed. E. Ragezino, Galleria Umberto · 'apoli 20639

▲ The *Commonwealth*, on this Hugo Lang card, was launched at Harland & Wolff in 1900 for the Dominion Line's Liverpool–Boston service. In 1903 the 12,097-ton vessel was transferred to White Star and renamed *Canopic*.

◄ A very popular vessel, the *Canopic* was employed on the Mediterranean service well into the start of the First World War. The message on this Ragezino card, posted 6 April 1908 from Boston to Bar Harbour, Maine, reads: *This is the steamer we sailed on … it reminded me of our visit last year on the battleship.* After serving under the Liner Requisition Scheme from 1917 to 1919, she continued on the Mediterranean service for three further years before returning to White Star's north Atlantic operations and was finally scrapped in South Wales in 1925.

HANDS ACROSS THE SEA.

ARABIC.

◄ The 15,801-ton *Arabic* had been laid down as the *Minnewaska* for the Atlantic Transport Line but was launched in 1902 as the *Arabic* for White Star. Employed primarily on the North Atlantic service, she made, after 1905, several spring cruises to the Mediterranean. This card by the Art Publishing Co. was posted at Liverpool on 20 May 1913 with the message: *Dear Bessie. Arrived at Liverpool 6.30. Cheer up. With love. H.G.* I don't think George V would have approved of his 'Royal Standard' being portrayed!

➤ 'Ginger' the cat was a popular member of *Arabic*'s crew, so much so that this Hodge postcard was sold on board. Whether *'our cat'* was written by a passenger or a member of the crew will never be known. This postcard was mailed at Alexandria on 16 March 1907 to Brixton. On 19 August 1915 the *Arabic* was torpedoed and sunk by U24 off the Old Head of Kinsale whilst en route to New York, with the loss of forty-four lives. This was White Star's first loss in the First World War and, coming so soon after the loss of Cunard's *Lusitania* in May of the same year, caused such outrage in the USA that Germany claimed her submarine was acting in self-defence! The *Arabic* sank in seven minutes but 390 people were saved. Sadly Ginger was not amongst the rescued.

PHOTO BY HODGE, BOSTON

"Ginger"
S.S.Arabic

" GINGER "
" S. S. ARABIC "

Our cat.

"S. S. CRETIC"

◄ Another vessel to be switched within the IMMC fleet was Leyland Line's *Hanoverian*. The 13,507-ton vessel was launched in 1902 but, after only three return transatlantic voyages and upon Leyland being acquired by IMMC, she was transferred to Dominion Line and renamed *Mayflower* in 1903. That same year she was transferred yet again, this time to White Star, and renamed *Cretic*. For the next six years she operated on the Mediterranean service and afterwards the North Atlantic. Following her war service, under the Liner Requisition Scheme, she joined *Canopic* back on the USA–Mediterranean route.

▼ *Cretic* re-joined Leyland Line in 1923 as *Devonian*, illustrated on this C.W. Hunt card, and operated on the North Atlantic carrying only 250 one-class (Cabin) passengers. She was scrapped at the Firth of Forth in 1929.

SOUVENIR OF VOYAGE.

S.S. "Baltic."

Commander - W. FINCH, (Lieut.-Com., R.N R Retd)

ABSTRACT OF LOG.

April	1	—	3-38 p.m. Depart Chibucto Head
,,	2	259	Moderate sea, foggy and overcast
,,	3	294	Moderate sea, dull, foggy and overcast
,,	4	291	Moderate sea, fine, clear and cloudy
,,	5	311	Moderate sea, fine, clear and cloudy
,,	6	337	Moderate sea, overcast to clear
,,	7	336	Moderate wind, swell, fine, overcast
,,	8	339	Moderate sea, fine and clear
,,	9	258	2-40 p m. arrive Rock Light,
	Total	2595	

Passage 7 days, 19 hours, 2 minutes

◄ The 23,876-ton *Baltic*, third vessel of the 'Big Four', was never as successful as her sisters. White Star had asked that Harland & Wolff increase her size but her engines, being the same as those of *Celtic* and *Cedric*, were not sufficiently capable of handling the additional tonnage resulting in a slower speed. She remained throughout her career on the Liverpool–New York service apart from her wartime duties as a troopship from 1915 to 1918. In 1927 she became the first of the 'Big Four' to be converted to 'Cabin' class with the removal of her first class. Unfortunately this 'Souvenir of Voyage' is not dated. The illustration shows *Baltic* at Liverpool with the tender *Magnetic* alongside.

➤ By the 1930s it was possible to have one's 'on board' photographs produced as postcards. The message on this card, mailed to the Isle of Man from the SS *Baltic* at New York on 11 October 1930, reads: *Dear Sister and Brother. Had a very rough passage up today. This is a snap of the storm. Everybody sick. I nearly went under myself. I have drunk no tea or coffee on board. Expect to land on Monday sometime. Love to all. Your Sister Nellie. Baltic* was scrapped at Osaka in 1933.

RMS Baltic in a Rough Sea

▲ *Baltic* at Queenstown. (Illustration by Norman Wilkinson)

▲ RMS *Adriatic* in Cherbourg Harbour. (Illustration by Norman Wilkinson)

▲ A John Adams Southampton card posted in November 1907 from New York to Switzerland. White Star's company pennant and funnel colours are prominent on the left of *Adriatic*.

▲ It was decided to place *Adriatic*, the fourth vessel of the 'Big Four', on the new Southampton–Cherbourg–New York service despite her maiden voyage, under the command of Captain E.J. Smith on 8 May 1907, being from Liverpool to New York, and she inaugurated the route in June of that year. This John Adams postcard commemorates the opening of the new route, aimed at capturing some of the continental European passenger market at Cherbourg.

▲ The 24,541-ton *Adriatic*, on this Real Photographs card, was launched at Harland & Wolff, Belfast on 20 September 1906 and was, briefly, the largest liner in the world at the time. Later that day Cunard's *Mauretania* was launched on the Tyne and captured the title!

S. S. ADRIATIC AT SOUTHAMPTON, JUNE 5TH 1907.

▲ *Adriatic* departs Southampton, for the first time, on 5 June 1907. After Cherbourg she would call at Queenstown, Ireland en route to New York. *Oceanic*, *Majestic* and *Teutonic* were also switched to the Southampton service.

∧ A Premier Co. postcard of *Adriatic* at Southampton mailed from that city on 3 June 1907, two days prior to her maiden departure. The message reads: *We went over this boat today, it is wonderful. Electric, Turkish and swimming baths & a gymnasium & everything just as though you were in a large hotel.* *Adriatic* was the first liner to feature a Turkish bath and indoor swimming pool. I wonder if the man sitting on the bollard is one of the 'we'?

∧ A Priestly & Sons card depicting *Adriatic* in dry dock. Note the fellow up a ladder by the rudder.

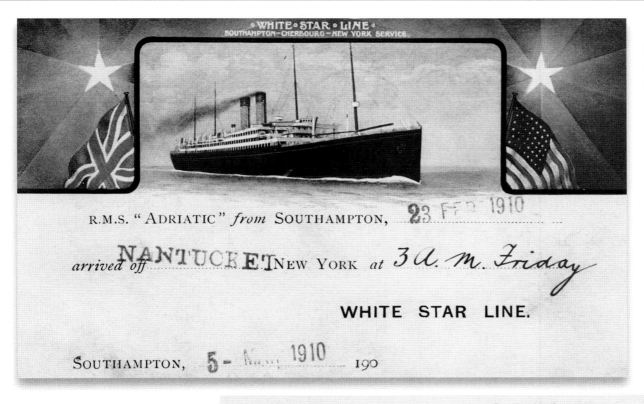

R.M.S. "ADRIATIC" *from* SOUTHAMPTON, 23 FEB 1910

arrived off NANTUCKET NEW YORK *at* 3 A. M. Friday

WHITE STAR LINE.

SOUTHAMPTON, 5 - May 1910 190

◄ A postcard, mailed by the White Star Line to a company in Essex, advising the safe arrival of the *Adriatic* off Nantucket. Posted from Southampton on 5 March 1910.

➤ *Adriatic* served as a troopship during the First World War and this card, issued by the Jewish Welfare Board, carries on the reverse the notification 'Soldiers Mail. No postage necessary if mailed on board or on dock' with spaces for Co…….. Reg……..…Div……… Going to camp………

S. S. Adriatic

© *Int. Film Service*

Greetings from the Jewish Welfare Board to Soldiers and Sailors of the U. S. Army and Navy

After her 1919 refit, during which her forward promenade deck was glazed in, the *Adriatic* resumed her transatlantic service rejoining her three sisters at Liverpool in 1922. This magnificent Jerome view of *Adriatic* in mid-ocean has her passing another vessel.

With the *Titanic*'s loss still fresh in the public's mind the sighting of an iceberg would have warranted a photograph. This was taken on 23 September 1919 from *Adriatic*.

PASSED BY THE
RMS "ADRIATIC"
SEP. 23ᵈ 1919

◄ In 1926 *Adriatic* began a series of winter cruises and two years later 'Cabin' class replaced first class. From 1929 she spent a considerable amount of time laid up, making only the occasional cruise. She is seen here, dressed overall, on one of her cruises with her gangway down and the wake of the departing tender is clearly visible in the foreground.

➤ A company-issued postcard illustrating the comforts of the 'Tourist Third Cabin Lounge' on board *Adriatic*. After White Star's merger with Cunard in 1934, *Adriatic* made only one more cruise and was scrapped at Osaka in 1935.

R.M.S. ADRIATIC - THE LOUNGE
TOURIST THIRD CABIN

WHITE STAR LINE

247 CHERBOURG. — *Le Transbordeur " Gallic "* . — ND *Phot.*

▲ With the introduction of the Cherbourg stopover in 1907, White Star purchased from the Corporation of Birkenhead the ferry *Birkenhead*, launched in 1894, for tender duties at the French port. The 461-ton paddle wheeler was renamed *Gallic*. This card was posted at Cherbourg on 29 April 1910.

209. - CHERBOURG. - Le Vapeur *Gallic* et le Port de Commerce

Collection P. B.

◄ A crowded *Gallic* at Cherbourg with the white star prominent on her paddle box. She could carry up to 1,200 passengers plus baggage on her decks. The card was posted in 1908 with, as was customary for the French postal service, the stamp affixed to the front.

► Awaiting her next tour of duty, *Gallic* rests at Cherbourg on this postcard by Au rendez-vous des Touristes, mailed on 15 September 1909. *Gallic* was replaced by the tenders *Nomadic* and *Traffic* in 1911 and returned to the Mersey in 1912 for occasional use as a baggage vessel before being scrapped at Garston in 1913.

CHERBOURG -- La Gare Maritime et les Navires Transbordeurs

Edit. «Au rendez-vous des Touristes»

➤ White Star purchased, in 1908, the three-masted sailing vessel *Mersey* for use as a training ship for up to eighty cadets. She had, since her launch in 1894, been employed on the UK–Calcutta route for the James Nourse Company. She is seen here at Liverpool 'during the King's visit' – whether Edward VII or George V is not mentioned!

(No 6.) WHITE STAR TRAINING SHIP "MERSEY", DURING THE KINGS VISIT TO L'POOL.

➤ The *Mersey* here shown at Newcastle NSW with an 'Afric' class vessel behind. The message, on this C.C. & Co. card posted to Jersey, reads: *There are over 50 large sailing vessels here now such as are on this card and over 100 are on their way to Newcastle NSW owing to the strikes at home there is a big demand for Newcastle coal. The place is like a forest of bare trees.*

King's Wharf, Newcastle.

CADET SHIP "MERSEY"   PHOTO BY CAPT CORNER

◄ During her six years with White Star the *Mersey* made six round-trip voyages from the UK to Australia via the Cape. She was possibly also the first sailing vessel to be equipped with radio. This card by Captain Corner, posted from Australia on 14 November 1909, carries the message: *This a photograph of the ship I am in with Clark. Just arrived in Sydney & am having a very good time. We may be going to Newcastle NSW next week but not if this great strike comes on. Mersey* was sold in 1915 and scrapped in Britain in 1923.

R.M.S. LAURENTIC.

▲ A magnificent view, by C.W. Hunt, of the 14,892-ton *Laurentic* displaying her classic Harland & Wolff profile. Commissioned by the White Star Line for the joint White Star-Dominion service to Canada, *Laurentic* was joined by her sister *Megantic*, and Dominion's *Canada* and *Dominion*, to provide a weekly service. *Laurentic* differed from her sister in that she had three propellers, the centre being driven by surplus steam from the outer two. *Megantic*'s propulsion was by the traditional two propellers. The triple-screw system was found to be the superior of the two and this method was later adopted for the giant 'Olympic' class liners.

LAURENTIC.

"THE LAURENTIC", LIVERPOOL.

S. S. LAURENTIC

New York, JAN 15 1913

The S. S "Laurentic" arrived at

Santiago

at *5 a.m.* to-day.

Yours very truly,

Cruise Department

⌃ The *Laurentic* had originally been laid down as the *Alberta* for the Dominion Line but was renamed prior to her launch for the White Star in September 1908. She is seen here in the Mersey being towed away from her berth by the tender *Magnetic*, whose stern can be seen on the left of the picture.

➤ Prior to the First World War *Laurentic* would cruise occasionally to the Caribbean. With this postcard, mailed to New Hampshire from New York on 15 January 1913, the cruise department advises Mrs Geo. Trittle of Hillsboro that *Laurentic* had arrived at Santiago (de Cuba).

"MEGANTIC" 14,878 Tons. Built 1908.

▲ The 14,878-ton *Megantic* was laid down at Harland & Wolff as the *Albany* for the Dominion Line but was renamed prior to her launch for White Star Line in December 1908. Her conventional twin-screw propulsion was less successful than her sister *Laurentic*'s triple-screw system. She is seen here being towed out into the Mersey on this Northern Publishing card.

WHITE STAR LINE CANADIAN SERVICE

S. S. "MEGANTIC"   15,000 TONS

◄ The classic Harland & Wolff profile is again evident in this postcard of *Megantic*. In 1926, with the closure of the Dominion Line, 'White Star Line Canadian Service' became the title of the operation.

➤ During the off season, in the early 1920s, *Megantic* was removed from the Canadian run and placed on cruising to the West Indies. Artist Montague Black (1884–1964) illustrates her here at Havana.

White Star Line, R.M.S. "Megantic" 14,878 tons, at Havana.

S·S MEGANTIC AT SEA WITH CANADIAN TROOPS.
FEB. 26. 1915

◄ At the outbreak of the First World War *Megantic* was, almost immediately, commandeered for trooping duties. She was refitted to accommodate 1,800 men and is seen here at sea, on this H. Wheeler card, with Canadian troops for Europe. After her post-war refit she resumed her Canadian service and was converted to 'Cabin' class in 1924. In February 1933 she departed the UK, with *Baltic*, for Osaka and demolition.

► In 1914 *Laurentic* was requisitioned as a troop transport for the Canadian Expeditionary Force but, in 1915, was converted into an armed merchant cruiser with seven 5.5-inch and three 4-inch guns. She is seen here in wartime grey paint as HMS *Laurentic*. On 25 January 1917, off Lough Swilly N.I., whilst en route to Halifax, she struck two mines and sank with £5 million of gold bullion being carried as payment to the Canadian government for munitions. Despite having got away from the sinking vessel, 354 men died of exposure in the open boats awaiting rescue. Most of the gold was recovered between 1919 and 1924.

HMS LAURENTIC.

CANADIAN PACIFIC S. S. "MONTROSE". Gross Tonnage 16,402.

▲ Both *Laurentic* and *Megantic* featured in the hunt for and arrest of Dr Hawley Crippen, wanted by Scotland Yard in connection with the murder of his wife 'Cora' in 1910. Crippen and his lover, Ethel 'Le Neve' Neave, fled the UK to Belgium and, with Le Neve disguised as a boy, boarded the Canadian Pacific liner *Montrose* sailing from Antwerp to Canada. Captain Kendall of the *Montrose*, later to command the ill-fated *Empress of Ireland*, became suspicious of the pair and telegraphed Scotland Yard. Chief Inspector Walter Dew, in charge of the case, took the faster *Laurentic* from Liverpool to Quebec and boarded the *Montrose* on 31 October as she entered the St Lawrence. It is believed that this was the first time that radio had been used to apprehend a criminal. Crippen and his lover were arrested and returned with Dew to the UK on board the *Megantic*. In two separate trials Le Neve was acquitted but Crippen was found guilty by a jury in less than half an hour and was hanged at Pentonville Prison in November 1910.

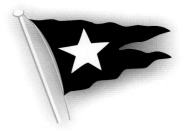

CHAPTER FOUR

1911 HOPES AND DREAMS

S.S. "ZEALANDIC"

▲ The 8,090-ton *Zealandic* was launched at Harland & Wolff in 1911 for the joint White Star-Shaw Savill service to New Zealand. She was designed to carry up to 1,000 emigrants outbound and return with a cargo of wool. After serving the British Government under the Liner Requisition Scheme she returned to the New Zealand service in 1919. The message on this card, written at sea on 19 July 1919, reads: *Just a few lines to let you know I am well on my way home. Left Tilbury on 3rd. inst. and should reach Capetown on Thursday. Weather has been fairly good up to date but owing to it being winter in the s. Hemisphere we can look forward to some ups and downs before reaching home. This vessel is travelling out without any cargo so rolls & dips at every opportunity. Unfortunately for me this is a family boat and turned out badly. I would advise no-one to travel by a family transport.* Zealandic was transferred in 1926 to the Aberdeen Line, renamed *Mamilius* and transferred again in 1932, under the name *Mamari*, to Shaw Savill. At the outbreak of the Second World War she was sold to the Admiralty who converted her into the 'dummy' aircraft carrier HMS *Hermes*. In June of 1941 she was torpedoed and sunk by a German E-boat off Cromer whilst en route to being converted back into a cargo vessel. The real HMS *Hermes* was lost on 9 April 1942.

The World's Greatest Gantry, in Harland & Wolff's North Shipyard, - Belfast.

▲ To compete with Germany's express transatlantic liners and Cunard's *Lusitania* and *Mauretania*, White Star decided in 1907 to plan the largest and most luxurious ships in the world. 'Size and comfort over speed' had long been company policy and the new vessels would continue that tradition. The keel of the first, *Olympic*, was laid down in December 1908 and the second, *Titanic*, less than four months later on 31 March 1909. We see here the two, side by side, at Harland & Wolff with *Olympic*, in a more advanced stage of completion, on the right. This postcard was issued to illustrate the enormous gantry that had been constructed to build the super-liners.

SURPASSING THE-GREATEST BUILDINGS AND MEMORIALS OF EARTH

The White Star Line's New Triple-screw Steamers
"OLYMPIC" ☆ "TITANIC"
LARGEST AND FINEST IN THE WORLD
(SEE OVER.)

◄ A promotional US card comparing White Star's new vessels with, from left to right: Bunker Hill Monument – Boston; Public Buildings – Philadelphia; Washington Monument – Washington DC; Metropolitan Tower – New York; New Woolworth Building – New York; Cologne Cathedral; Great Pyramid – Giza; St Peter's – Rome.

➤ A second promotional postcard, again issued in the US, featuring an artist's impression of one of the two, at the time, identical vessels.

The Largest and Finest Steamers in the world
WHITE STAR LINE
"OLYMPIC" ☆ "TITANIC"
882½ FEET LONG   45,000 TONS REGISTER   92½ FEET BROAD

Liner on Stocks, Harland & Wolff's Shipyard, Belfast.

▲ A Walton of Belfast card shows *Olympic* on the stocks prior to her launch with her hull painted grey for the occasion.

➤ 20 October 1910 and, reaching a speed of 12mph, *Olympic*'s hull takes to the water portrayed here on another Walton card. As was customary with the launching of White Star's vessels at Harland & Wolff, there were no formal naming ceremonies with champagne etc. The workforce were given time off to witness the launch, a rocket was fired and the ship slid into the water before a group of invited dignitaries.

Launch of the White Star Liner "Olympic," the largest vessel in the world, October 20th, 1910.   WALTON, PUBLISHER

BOW VIEW, "OLYMPIC" DOCKED IN NEW GRAVING DOCK, BELFAST IST APRIL 1911
DISPLACEMENT OF VESSEL, 33,000 TONS.

▲ *Olympic* in the new graving dock at Harland & Wolff. Note the large crane on the right. Manufactured in Germany, it had been acquired for the 'fitting out' of the giant new vessels.

➤ A Doherty & Son card shows *Titanic*, the second of the giant trio, launched at Belfast on 31 May 1911 the same day that her sister *Olympic* departed for Liverpool and Southampton. The gap in the construction of the two ships had grown, eventually, to nine months as men were transferred from *Titanic* to *Olympic*.

Launching of the "Titanic"—the Largest Vessel in the world—at Queen's Island, Belfast, May, 1911.

Length over all	...	...	...	882 feet 9 ins.	Distance from top of Funnel to Keel	175 feet 0 ins.
Breadth ,,	...	...	...	99 ,, 6 ,,	Number of Steel Decks, 11. Weight of Rudder, 100 tons.	
Height from Keel to Boat deck	...	...	97 ,, 4 ,,	Published by Doherty & Son, Ann St Belfast	

◄ Prior to her maiden voyage, whilst en route to Southampton from Belfast, *Olympic* made a courtesy call at Liverpool, her port of registry, on 1 June 1911, and was open to public inspection. The message on this Carbonora card, posted to Antwerp from Liverpool on 13 July 1911, reads: *This is a picture of the largest ship in the world, photographed in the river at Liverpool.*

3720 A

WHITE STAR S.S. OLYMPIC.
LENGTH 882½ft., BREADTH 92½ft., GROSS TONNAGE 45,000, 30,000 I.H.P.

ROTARY PHOTO, E.C.

▲ The 45,324-ton *Olympic* departed Southampton on her maiden voyage to New York, via Cherbourg and Queenstown, on 14 June 1911. The original design of the vessels had called for three funnels but a rear fourth was added for galley smoke and steam and to enhance the image, as shown on this Rotary card. To comply with British Board of Trade regulations, *Olympic* carried fourteen large wooden lifeboats each with a capacity of sixty-five persons, two small cutters, each with a forty-person capacity, and in addition four collapsible boats designed to fit into the davits after the cutters had been launched. Passenger accommodation was allocated to 1,054 first, 510 second and 1,020 third class, with a crew of 860.

La Basse Normandie Pittoresque

3151. Cherbourg (Manche) – Le Transbordeur "NOMADIC" à sa rentrée d'Escale - Au loin, Fort et Montagne du Roul

◄ The 1,273-ton *Nomadic* was one of two vessels built at Harland & Wolff for White Star, to act as tender at Cherbourg to their liners, replacing the ageing *Gallic*. Carrying up to 1,000 first- and second-class passengers, *Nomadic* worked at Cherbourg until 1940. At the fall of France she was employed by the British Navy based on the South Coast until 1945 when she returned to France. *Nomadic* is currently being restored at Belfast as the last remaining White Star vessel afloat. This Le Goubey card was mailed at Cherbourg on 13 June 1921.

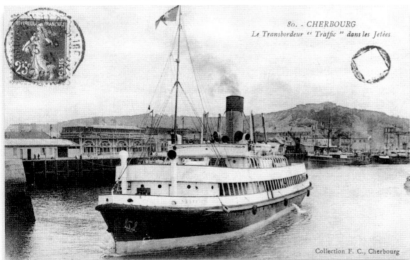

8o. - CHERBOURG
Le Transbordeur " Traffic " dans les Jetées

Collection F. C., Cherbourg

Embarking Passengers, Queenstown

▲ The 675-ton *Traffic*, portrayed on this F.C. Cherbourg card, accompanied *Nomadic* and *Olympic* from Belfast on 31 May 1911 and the two tenders proceeded directly to Cherbourg to await *Olympic*'s first visit. *Traffic* was designed to carry third-class passengers and baggage. Whilst in German hands, *Traffic* was sunk by the British in the English Channel on 17 January 1941.

▲ Tendering duties at Queenstown (Cobh) were undertaken by the paddle steamers *America* and *Ireland*, seen here at the White Star Line wharf on this card by Valentine of Dublin. They flew the flag of the company whose vessel they were attending at the time.

▲ *Olympic* makes her maiden arrival at New York on 21 June 1911, the only vessel of the trio so to do!

➤ An S. Cribb card, showing the crumpled bow of HMS *Hawke* after she had rammed *Olympic*. The White Star Line was blamed at the inquiry, which claimed that *Olympic*'s size and speed caused a suction effect. This despite *Hawke* being outside the distance laid down by the Admiralty! White Star appealed to the House of Lords but to no avail. *Olympic* returned to Belfast for six weeks of repairs.

THE CAVITY IN THE "OLYMPIC" AFTER THE COLLISION.
20 SEP: 1911. SILK 6.

➤ *Olympic* was badly damaged in collision with the Royal Navy cruiser HMS *Hawke* on 20 September in the Solent. The message on this 'Reginald Silk' card, posted 26 September 1911, reads: *Dear Jack. I sent you, in the Summer, a picture of this boat after I had seen her leave for New York. This is the hole she suffered in the collision with HMS Hawke last week. There was a bigger one below the water line. A man had just got up for lunch otherwise he would have been killed. Dads.*

.S CRIBB 7.

THE SOLENT COLLISION.
HMS HAWKE RETURNING TO HARBOUR
AFTER THE TERRIFIC IMPACT WITH THE OLYMPIC"

A WORLD'S RECORD.   ONE THIRD OF A MILE OF IRON & STEEL IN TWO SHIPS.
THE NEW WHITE STAR LINERS "OLYMPIC" & "TITANIC" AT BELFAST.

▲ *Olympic* returned again to Harland & Wolff on 1 March 1912 for the replacement of a lost propeller blade. *Titanic*, on the right of this Walton card, was moved from her 'fitting out' dock to allow *Olympic*'s entry and repair which lasted six days. Thus the scheduled maiden voyage of *Titanic* was delayed from 20 March to 10 April 1912.

The Sinking of H.M.S. "Audacious" in the Irish Sea, by a German Mine, during the Great War - 1914.
Abrahams & Sons
Devonport. 699

▼ The British battleship HMS *Audacious* sinking in the Irish Sea on 27 October 1914 after having struck a mine laid by the German liner *Berlin* (later to become White Star's third *Arabic*). This photograph by Abrahams & Sons was taken from *Olympic*, which had gone to the assistance of the warship and, using her lifeboats, rescued the crew of the doomed battleship.

➤ *Olympic* was immediately taken over for trooping duties at the outbreak of the First World War. This card, posted at Ottawa on 5 June 1916 to Ontario, carries the message: *Dear Friend. Just to let you know we are about to sail. Came on board Wednesday morning. Will send you a letter when I arrive in England. Bye.* Also on the reverse are the official stamps ON ACTIVE SERVICE and INTELLIGENCE OFFICE – HALIFAX FORTRESS.

CANADIAN EXPEDITIONARY FORCE
CANADA TO ENGLAND, JUNE, 1916
For Peace, Justice and Freedom.   *God Save the King.*

➤ HMS *Olympic* in wartime dazzle camouflage paint. She carried 6-inch guns and flew the Royal Navy's White Ensign.

▼ On 12 May 1918 the troopship *Olympic* rammed and sank the German submarine U103 off the Lizard having survived a torpedo attack and this was probably the only occasion that a passenger liner sank a U-boat! *Olympic* is seen here at Halifax NS returning US and Canadian troops at the end of the First World War. During this period she earned the nickname 'Old Reliable'. Throughout her war career she transported over 200,000 troops and travelled over 180,000 miles.

WHITE STAR LINE TRIPLE SCREW S. S. "OLYMPIC"

46,439 TONS LARGEST OIL BURNING STEAMER 882½ FEET LONG

◄ *Olympic* returned to Belfast for a major refit in August 1919 during which she was converted from coal to oil burning. In addition to removing the dirty business of 'coaling' this conversion reduced her engine room staff from 246 to sixty. This postcard carries, on the reverse, the company's advertisement 'The White Star Line's Triple Screw SS *Olympic*, largest British Steamer, plies between New York, Cherbourg and Southampton, making expeditious connections for all parts of Europe'. Note the post-*Titanic* increase in lifeboat capacity!

▼ *Olympic* making one of her many arrivals in the Hudson River with Manhattan Island to starboard. Sadly she would be the only vessel of the planned trio to make the transatlantic crossing for which they were intended.

Gymnasium, R.M.S. " Olympic."

◄ The first-class gymnasium on board *Olympic* featured here on a postcard, issued by the company, mailed 28 January 1926. There had been little change, if any, since 1912 and *Titanic*'s gymnasium would have been identical.

➤ Another company-issued card featuring, this time, the Turkish bath also for the use of first-class passengers. The advertisement on the reverse reads: 'The White Star Liner *Olympic* is the largest triple screw steamer in the world. A ship of 46,439 tons register, 882 feet in length, 92 feet in breadth and 105 feet in depth. She is associated with the '*Majestic*' and '*Homeric*' in maintaining the Company's Express Mail and Passenger Service between Southampton, Cherbourg and New York.'

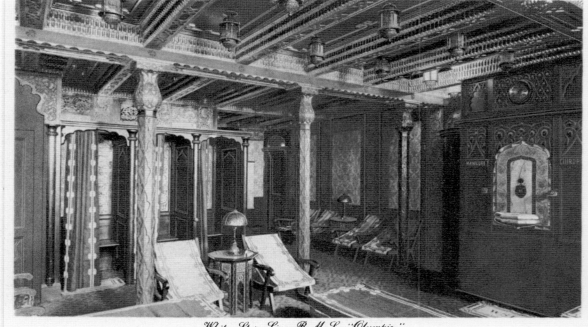

White Star Line R.M.S. "Olympic."
First-Class Turkish Bath.

S.17738. WHITE STAR LINE R.M.S. "OLYMPIC" 46,439 TONS.
FIRST CLASS LOUNGE & CINEMA.

◄ Much later in her career, the chairs in *Olympic*'s first-class lounge have been re-arranged to form a cinema as portrayed on this Kingsway postcard.

➤ With the introduction of Tourist Class in 1928, the *Olympic*'s third-class lounge is transformed into the Tourist Third Cabin Lounge on another Kingsway card.

S.17742. WHITE STAR LINE R.M.S. "OLYMPIC" 46,439 TONS.
TOURIST THIRD CABIN LOUNGE.

WHITE STAR LINE.

THIRD CLASS.

R.M.S. "OLYMPIC."   MAY 20, 1913

BREAKFAST.

HOMINY & MILK

CREAMED SALT COD   JACKET POTATOES

VEGETABLE STEW

FRESH BREAD & BUTTER

MARMALADE   SWEDISH BREAD

TEA   COFFEE

DINNER.

PEA SOUP

CORNED BRISKET OF BEEF AND CABBAGE

BAKED POTATOES

FRESH BREAD   CABIN BISCUITS

SAGO PUDDING

TEA.

FRESH FRIED FISH

FRESH BREAD & BUTTER

SWEDISH BREAD   MARMALADE

STEWED GREENGAGES & RICE

TEA

SUPPER

BISCUITS & CHEESE

... respecting the Food supplied, want of attention
... uld be at once reported to the Purser or Chief
... urposes of identification, each Steward wears a
... the arm.

WHITE STAR LINE.

THIRD CLASS

R.M.S. "OLYMPIC." - SEPTEMBER 6th, 1922.

BREAKFAST. -

Rolled Oats with Milk

Finnon Haddie

Broiled Sausages, Mashed Potatoes

Fresh Bread   Marmalade   Tea   Coffee

DINNER.

Vegetable Soup

Boiled Codfish, Egg Sauce

Roast Mutton, Onion Sauce

Carrots and Turnips   Boiled and Roast Potatoes

Bread and Butter Pudding

TEA. -

Rabbit and Ham Pie

Cold Roast Lamb and Morta Della Sausage

Mixed Pickles   Cheese   Potato Salad

Compote of Figs   Currant Buns

Preserves   Fresh Bread   Tea

SUPPER—Biscuits   Cheese   Gruel

Any complaint respecting the Food supplied, want of
attention, or incivility, should be at once reported to
the Purser or Chief Steward.

▲ With just over a year to go before the outbreak of the First World War, *Titanic* having sunk the previous year and the third sister not yet complete, this third-class menu for *Olympic* on 20 May 1913 carries the advertisement on the reverse, 'The Largest Steamer in the World'.

▲ Nine years later and *Olympic*'s third-class menu offers a greater and, possibly healthier, bill of fare. The reverse carries the company's advertisement for RMS *Majestic* (completing) 56,000 tons, RMS *Olympic* 46,439 tons and RMS *Homeric* 34,692 tons.

FAREWELL OF R.M.S. OLYMPIC FROM SOUTHAMPTON, 11ᵗʰ OCT. 1935.   PHOTO: J.M.P. HOOLEY.

▲ *Olympic*'s transatlantic schedule had been reduced by 1929 and she was employed on short cruises to Halifax NS from New York. In 1934, with the merger of White Star and Cunard, *Olympic* passed into the ownership of the new 'Cunard White Star Line'. That same year she collided with and sank the Nantucket lightship with the loss of eight of that vessel's crew. *Olympic* made her last crossing of the Atlantic from New York on 27 March 1935, after which she was laid up at Southampton, from where she departed, as portrayed by J.M.P. Hooley, on 11 October to be broken up at Jarrow. Her arrival on the north-east coast created work for many of the unemployed at this depressed time. The hull of *Olympic*, cut almost to the waterline, was towed to Inverkeithing for final breaking up.

WHITE STAR
LINE

R.M.S. "ZEELAND"
leaving Liverpool

S. S. NORTHLAND.

▲ The 11.905-ton *Zeeland*, built by John Brown & Co. on Clydebank in 1900 for the Red Star Line's transatlantic service from Antwerp, was transferred within IMMC to White Star in April 1910 to replace the lost *Republic*. Upon *Olympic*'s entry into service *Zeeland* was returned to Red Star, but after the wartime closure of Antwerp, she reverted to White Star ownership once more. This card was mailed on 1 December 1911.

➤ *Zeeland*'s name, sounding too Germanic, was changed to *Northland* in 1915, as was her sister *Vaderland* renamed *Southland*. This 'crossed-hands' card was mailed from the ship on 22 July 1915 before *Northland* was requisitioned for trooping later that year.

Transatlantique " Zeland "

Collection F. C. Cherbourg

◄ *Northland*, on another F.C. Cherbourg card, was converted to oil burning during her post-war refit in 1920. Her name reverted to *Zeeland* and she returned to Red Star's Antwerp–New York service.

➤ The final name change, to *Minnesota*, took place in 1927 when *Zeeland* was sold, again within the IMMC, to the Atlantic Transport Line for use on their London to New York service. She is seen here departing New York, as depicted by artist Charles Dixon (1872–1934), in her final colours. *Minnesota* was scrapped at Inverkeithing in 1930.

ATLANTIC TRANSPORT LINE

S.S. MINNESOTA. 11,904 TONS.

CHAPTER FIVE

DISASTER!

⌃ The morning of 4 April 1912 and the citizens of Southampton awoke to find that the world's largest liner had arrived during the night from Belfast, prior to her maiden voyage. As late as March that year the White Star Line had arranged for *Titanic*'s forward first-class promenade deck to be enclosed, as a result of complaints from passengers on board her sister *Olympic* of excess spray. There had been no courtesy call at Liverpool en route from Belfast as her departure had been delayed by strong winds.

WHITE STAR LINER 'TITANIC.
LEAVING SOUTHAMPTON DOCKS.
APRIL 10ᵀᴴ 1912.

X-MILLS
PHOTO.

> *Titanic* departed Southampton on her maiden voyage at 12 noon on Wednesday 10 April 1912. The liner *New York*, the two funnels of which can be seen behind the stern of *Titanic*, was moored alongside *Oceanic* to the left of the picture. *Titanic*'s suction and displacement caused the *New York* to snap her moorings and drift towards *Titanic*. Tugs assisting the great ship's departure managed to push *New York* away as *Titanic* stopped her engines, thus avoiding a collision. The message on the reverse of this 'Max-Mills' card reads: *Dear Maud. I thought perhaps you would like to have a photo of the boat. This is the best one taken as she was leaving the Docks. Hope you are feeling better. With love from Len.*

> Had it not been for the delay at Southampton, there would probably have been many more photographs of the *Titanic* taken at Cherbourg. As it was, dusk was falling by the time *Titanic* arrived. *Nomadic* and *Traffic* delivered their passengers and baggage at 7 p.m. and night had fallen as the *Titanic* departed for the overnight passage to Queenstown, as evident here in this P.B. Cherbourg card.

Le « Titanic » en rade de Cherbourg le soir du 10 avril 1912

Collection P. B., Cherbourg

◄ A company-issued postcard mailed to France from the UK on 16 December 1911, unsigned by the artist, hailing *Olympic* and *Titanic* as the 'Largest Steamers in the World'. This card would later be reissued showing only *Olympic*'s name.

➤ A colourful illustration of both *Olympic* and *Titanic* as depicted by artist Montague Black (1884–1940) on this company-issued postcard.

White Star Liner, "TITANIC."

◄ This rather naïve image of *Titanic*, with the White Star Line logo top left, would have been sold on board. This card, printed by National for the White Star Line, was re-published later with details of the ship's loss printed below the name.

➤ Many postcards purporting to show *Titanic* did, in fact, feature her sister *Olympic*. Until the decision to enclose *Titanic*'s forward promenade deck, having been taken only a few weeks before her maiden departure, the two vessels would have been almost identical.

1830   White Star Line R. M. S. Titanic

"Titanic. triple Screw, 45,000 tons,
Largest Steamer in the World."

➤ The message on the reverse of this card, mailed from Paynes Hotel, Southampton reads: *Arrived alright now going aboard. Goodbye William* and prompts the reader to believe William was boarding the *Titanic*. The postmark however is 23 April 1912, thirteen days after *Titanic*'s departure and eight days after her foundering. With the aid of the 1911 census and genealogical research it was discovered that William George Thomas, a nineteen-year-old granite quarry labourer, had posted this card to his aunt Janey Toy in Cornwall, prior to boarding the Cunard liner *Ultonia* which departed Southampton for Quebec on 23 April 1912. It is possible that William purchased this card carrying the 'present tense' wording prior to his departure from Cornwall and *Titanic*'s loss, and had written the address in ink with the intention of completing the message side, which he did in pencil, later.

"TITANIC" LIFEBOAT APPROACHING "CARPATHIA"

J. W. Barker, Copyright.

▲ At 11.40p.m. on the night of Sunday 14 April 1912 RMS *Titanic* collided with an iceberg and sank two hours and forty minutes later with the loss of over 1,500 lives. Within a couple of hours of *Titanic*'s foundering, the Cunard liner *Carpathia* had arrived on the scene and begun the rescue of over 700 survivors from the lifeboats. Lifeboat number 6, seen here approaching the *Carpathia* on this J. W. Barker card, was lowered from the port side of the *Titanic* at 12.55a.m. Standing at the tiller is Quartermaster Robert Hichens who had been at the wheel of the *Titanic* at the time of the collision. Amongst the twenty-eight passengers and crew are Lookouts Frederick Fleet, the first to sight the berg, and Archie Jewell, Mrs J.J. (Molly) Brown of Denver and Canadian Major Arthur Peuchen who slid down the boat's falls, when asked by Second Officer Lightoller to assist the boat's crew. Lifeboat number 6 had a capacity of sixty-five!

The arrival of ''S. S. Carpathia'' after the disaster - April

1912

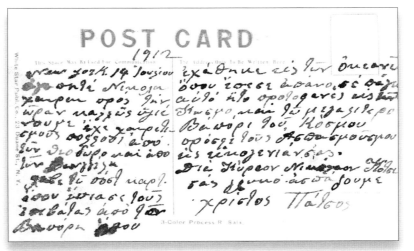

POST CARD

1912

3-Color Process R. Sala.

<< A contemporary American postcard depicting the *Carpathia*'s rescue. The message on this card, written in Greek and mailed from New York on 14 July 1912, reads: *We're all right for now Mr Nick. Greetings and best wishes to you all from myself, Uncle Theo and Auntie Angela. This is a postcard of the boat which rescued the people from the largest boat in the world, lost on the ocean. It crashed onto ice and sank. Who would have thought that? Amazing! Best wishes to you and your family, Mr Nicholas. Christos Patsos.*

R.M.S. TITANIC

ROYAL JUBILEE HALL
WEYMOUTH.
WEEK COMMENCING NOV. 9th, 1914
6.0.   TWICE NIGHTLY   8.15.
Matinees Wednesday & Saturday at 3 o'clock

POST CARD.

CHARLES W. & JOHN R. POOLE'S
GIGANTIC REPRODUCTION ILLUSTRATIVE
OF THE
LOSS of the "TITANIC"
The Immortal Tale of Simple Heroism

In Eight Tableaux, comprising :—
1. A splendid marine effect of the Gigantic Vessel gliding from the Quayside at Southampton.
2. Cork Harbour, showing the return of the White Star Tender to Queenstown and the "Titanic" outward bound.
3. MID-OCEAN. The "Titanic," brilliantly illuminated, speeding along at 21 knots.
4. The S.S. "Touraine" in the icefield, and carefully steering her way through the towering bergs.
5. The approach of the iceberg. The collision and grinding crash. Lowering out the lifeboats.
6. FOUNDERING. The great vessel sinking by the head. The extinction of the lights. The Sinking.
7. The arrival of the "Carpathia" and rescue of the survivors.
8. The Vision.

THE ADDRESS ONLY TO BE
WRITTEN HERE

STAMP

The spectacle staged in its entirety by John R Poole, and every endeavour made to convey a true pictorial idea of the whole history of the disaster. Unique Mechanical and Electric Effects, special music and the story described in a thrilling manner

▲< An illustration of *Titanic* (*Olympic*) by artist William Frederick Mitchell (1845–1914) from an original watercolour drawing, printed and published by J. Salmon of Sevenoaks. This card has been overprinted to advertise the Poole Bros' staging of the disaster in eight tableaux at the Royal Jubilee Hall Weymouth in November 1914.

'THE TITANIC' S. S.; 882 ft. long; the largest boat in the world; sunk April 15, 1912, at 2:20 A. M.; on her maiden trip; with a loss of about 1,500 passengers.

▲ Another *Titanic* (*Olympic*) image. This time a photograph, with *Titanic*'s name amateurishly printed on the bow, by the Kraus Mfg. Co. Postmarked 1912, a postcard manufacturer is inviting orders of the card at 75 cents per 100 as well as a book of the disaster for a nett price of 50 cents.

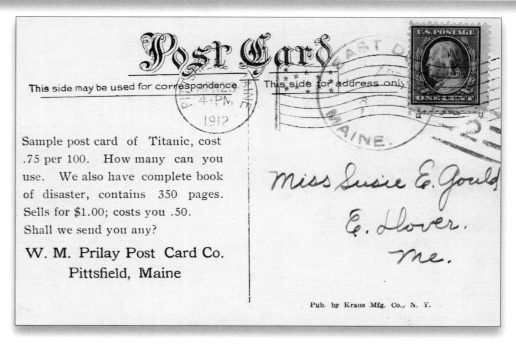

Post Card

This side may be used for correspondence. This side for address only.

Sample post card of Titanic, cost .75 per 100. How many can you use. We also have complete book of disaster, contains 350 pages. Sells for $1.00; costs you .50. Shall we send you any?

W. M. Prilay Post Card Co. Pittsfield, Maine

Miss Susie E. Gould,
E. Dover.
Me.

Pub. by Kraus Mfg. Co., N. Y.

▲ Following the disaster to the *Titanic*, many 'in memoriam' cards were issued. This National postcard, mailed from Southampton a month later on 15 May 1912, depicts a naïve image of the ship and Captain E. J. Smith (lost in the sinking). Also shown are the words and music to the hymn 'Nearer my God to Thee' which, it is claimed, was heard from the ship's orchestra playing out on deck during the evacuation. The message on the card reads: *Dearest M & T. You see where we are … Am sending you a card of the ship. Oh the poor widows we keep meeting. Love Flo.*

CHAPTER SIX

WAR AND PEACE

▲ The 9,748-ton *Belgic* only served the White Star Line for two years from 1911 to 1913 on the Liverpool to Australia service. Built by the N.Y. Shipbuilding Corp. of NJ in 1903 as the *Mississippi* for the Atlantic Transport Line, she and her sister *Massachusetts* were entitled to display the US flag. *Mississippi* was designed to carry cattle on the eastbound transatlantic journey and emigrants on the return. In 1906 she was transferred to Red Star Line and renamed *Samland*. At the time of her transfer to White Star her tonnage had increased to 10,151 and she was refitted to accommodate 1,800 third-class passengers. In 1913 she reverted to Red Star Line, was renamed *Samland* again and resumed her Antwerp–New York service. The message on this, crossed-hands, State Series card reads: *This is a picture of the boat we are in it is not very beautiful but if it takes us over that is the main thing.* *Belgic* was scrapped at Ghent in 1931.

▲ *Britannic* was the third vessel of the 'Olympic' trio and the second White Star ship to bear the name. Her completion was delayed by the Court of Enquiry into the loss of her sister-ship *Titanic*. She is seen here prior to her launch at Belfast.

▲ 26 February 1914: the launch of *Britannic*. There has been some suggestion that her name was to have been *Gigantic*, and that it was changed after *Titanic*'s loss, but there is no real evidence to confirm this. This card was posted in Battersea on 18 May 1920.

◀ The *Britannic* in White Star colours as she would have appeared prior to the outbreak of the First World War. Note the lattice gantry davits capable of lowering four lifeboats at the same time.

THE NEW WHITE STAR LINER "BRITANNIC."

THE LARGEST BRITISH BUILT VESSEL.   GROSS TONNAGE 50,000.   LENGTH 900 FEET.   BREADTH 94 FEET.   TOTAL HEIGHT FROM
KEEL TO NAVIGATING BRIDGE 104 FEET 6 INCHES.   ACCOMMODATION 2,600 PASSENGERS, 950 CREW.

⋀ Another Walton of Belfast card, portraying a heavily doctored image of an 'Olympic' class liner. Note the added 'drawn-in' lifeboats intended to depict the *Britannic* as she would have appeared in White Star service. At the outbreak of the First World War, whilst fitting out, *Britannic* was converted into a hospital ship with 3,300 beds. A year was to go by before a decision was made to use her in that capacity.

BRITANNIC

◄ In December 1915 the 48,158-ton 'His Majesty's Hospital Ship' *Britannic* made her maiden voyage from Belfast to Alexandria. With a green band round her white-painted hull she had three large red crosses on each side. Her funnels, slightly shorter than those of her sisters, were painted a buff colour without White Star's black tops.

❯ HMHS *Britannic* in Mudros Harbour about to commence her last journey back to the UK. During her career she made a total of five round-trip voyages to Mudros returning to either Marseilles or Southampton.

H.M. HOSPITAL SHIP "BRITANNIC."

⌃ An artist's impression of HMHS *Britannic* on this card posted at Southampton on 10 February 1916 to Essex, almost certainly from a patient. The card carries, on the reverse, the official stamp ON ACTIVE SERVICE and the message, written on 8 February, reads: *On board the SS Britanic. Dear Barney & Doley. Just a line to let you know that I am on board the above ship. I expect to arrive at Southampton tomorrow Wednesday. I am fairly well & hope you are the same. Will let you know where I go to. Your Brother. Tom Shadrack.*

H.M. HOSPITAL SHIP "BRITANNIC."

▲ Another artist's impression of *Britannic* as a hospital ship. There is no stamp or postmark but the message on this card, mailed to Burton-on-Trent, reads: *HMHS Britannic c/o FPO. This is the boat, we came on board yesterday and are anchored off the Isle of Wight at present. I expect we shall be off today. The boats we went to Malta and back on are babies compared with this. She is about the largest ship afloat & is an American liner really!* Just after 8a.m. on 21 November 1916, in the Zea Channel off mainland Greece, the *Britannic* struck a mine and sank an hour later with the loss of twenty-eight lives, but over 1,000 survivors were rescued by the escorting warships. The *Britannic* remains to this day one of the largest wartime losses in the British Merchant Navy.

◄ The triple-screw, 18,481-ton *Ceramic* joined the White Star-S.S.A. joint service to New Zealand in 1913 and was, for the next ten years, the largest vessel on the route. In 1914 she was requisitioned, as HMAT A40, to bring the Australian Expeditionary Force to the UK and, whilst serving under the Liner Requisition Scheme from 1917 to 1919, survived several submarine attacks.

▲ *Ceramic*, passing under the partially built Sydney Harbour Bridge on 6 October 1930. The bridge was opened in 1932, work having commenced in December 1928.

▲ After the merger of White Star with Cunard, *Ceramic* passed, with *Ionic*, into the ownership of Shaw Savill & Albion in 1934. She underwent a refit and modernisation at Harland & Wolff's Govan yard in 1936 during which her forward bridge deck and new verandah café aft were glazed in, as reflected in this Real Photographs image. At the outbreak of the Second World War, *Ceramic* was retained on her original service via Cape Town but also carried military personnel. She was torpedoed and sunk on 7 December 1942, off the Azores, by U515 with the loss of 278 crew and 378 passengers. There was one survivor!

◄ Red Star Line's *Lapland* was, at her launch in June 1908, the largest vessel to fly the Belgian flag. The 17,540-ton liner operated from Antwerp to New York via Dover and was famous for bringing home the surviving crew members of the *Titanic* in 1912 after their release from the US Court of Enquiry. These survivors disembarked at Plymouth after a crossing in third class during which they were isolated from the press.

▼ At the fall of Belgium in 1914 *Lapland* was, with *Zeeland* and *Vaderland*, transferred to the White Star Line. In 1917 she was commandeered under the Liner Requisition Scheme as a troopship with a capacity of 3,000. She is seen here in dazzle-paint camouflage. At the end of the First World War she reverted to White Star's transatlantic service but, with the release of *Olympic* from wartime duties, was returned to Red Star's Antwerp–New York service via Southampton. *Lapland* was scrapped in Japan in 1934.

▲ Built at Harland & Wolff, Belfast for the Holland America Line, the 32,234-ton *Statendam* was purchased by the British Government for conversion to a troopship in 1917. Now named *Justicia*, it was planned that she would be a replacement for Cunard's lost *Lusitania*. White Star had, however, sufficient crew available from their lost *Britannic* so *Justicia* passed into their management on 7 April 1917. This Nautical Photo Agency card shows her here as a troopship in wartime grey. Her rear funnel was a dummy for ventilation purposes.

➤ On 19 July 1918 the now dazzle-painted *Justicia* was torpedoed by UB64 off the Hebrides. With the majority of her crew taken off, the damaged ship was taken in tow by one of her escorting vessels, HMS *Sonia*. In the morning of the next day *Justicia* was again torpedoed, this time by U124, and sank three hours later with the loss of sixteen lives. Harland & Wolff built a near-replica *Statendam* for Holland America Line in 1921.

◄ With an urgent need for replacement tonnage, White Star's fourth *Belgic* was hurriedly launched in 1917 as the *Belgenland* for the Red Star Line. She was completed as a cargo vessel with two funnels and three masts and renamed *Belgic*. Although initially delivered in dazzle-paint camouflage, she was converted in 1918 into a troopship with a capacity of 3,000 and is seen here in Red Star Line colours engaged in troop repatriation duties.

▼ *Belgic* returned to Harland & Wolff in March 1922 for completion to her original design and is seen here, in this Real Photographs card, as Red Star's *Belgenland*, a 24,547-ton passenger liner with three funnels. During this rebuild she was also converted to oil burning. In 1935 *Belgenland* was sold to the Atlantic Transport Line and renamed *Columbia* but, after an unsuccessful attempt at cruising out of New York to the West Indies, was scrapped at Bo'ness, Firth of Forth in 1936.

S.S. "VEDIC"

◄ The 9,332-ton *Vedic* was probably intended, in 1913 planning, for Red Star's European emigrant service but was built by Harland & Wolff Govan in 1918 as a troopship. After the launch the hull was towed to Belfast for completion. *Vedic* entered service for White Star from Glasgow to Boston in December. She repatriated 1,000 British troops from Russia in 1919 who had initially been dispatched to aid with fighting the revolutionaries. After her 1920 refit *Vedic* settled down to work White Star's UK to Canada emigrant service. This card, posted from Quebec on 9 May 1921, carries the message: *Ship rolling. On board Tuesday. Dear Will & Jennie and all. Splendid everything up till now. Expect arrive Quebec Sunday. Write again on arrival. Love to all from Chris & Ethel.*

➤ *Vedic* was refitted in 1925 for the Liverpool to Australia emigrant service. This Kingsway card was posted in December with the message: *SS Vedic Dear Aunt. Just arrived on board rather cold. Will write later & tell you how we got on. With love Ethel & Jack.* Vedic, the first White Star liner with a cruiser stern, was laid up in 1930 and finally scrapped at Rosyth in 1934, being surplus to Cunard White Star requirements.

S.15108.   WHITE STAR LINE S. S. "VEDIC". 9.332 TONS.

◄ White Star's second *Gallic* was launched at Worman Clark's Belfast yard in 1918 as *War Argus*. The 7,914-ton vessel was one of twenty-two built for the Shipping Controller. White Star purchased *War Argus* in 1919 for their Australian cargo service and she was renamed *Gallic*.

▼ *Gallic* was sold to the Clan Line in 1933 and renamed *Clan Colquhoun*. Having survived the Second World War she was eventually scrapped in Hong Kong in 1956.

S.S. "CLAN COLQUHOUN."

∧ Another G-type vessel built for the Shipping Controller, the *War Priam* was sold to White Star whilst fitting out at Harland & Wolff, Belfast, and renamed *Bardic* in 1919. Whilst serving White Star's Australian cargo service she ran aground near the Lizard on 31 August 1924. This F.E. Gibson card shows the Cornish lifeboat returning from the stranded vessel.

Wreck SS "Bardic"

◀ A Hawke of Helston card with a dramatic stern view of the stranded *Bardic*.

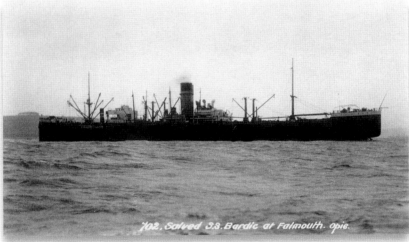

702. Salved S.S. Bardic at Falmouth. Opie.

▲ The *Bardic* was, after nearly a month aground, finally refloated on 29 September. The severely damaged vessel returned to Harland & Wolff for repair. The salvaged *Bardic* is seen here at Falmouth on this Opie card.

▲ After several owners and name changes, John Latsis of Piraeus purchased and renamed the vessel *Marathon* in 1937. She was sunk by the German battlecruiser *Scharnhorst* on 9 March 1941 whilst a convoy straggler off the Cape Verde Islands. Her distress radio message and destruction allowed the bulk of the convoy to escape a similar fate.

ZEPPELIN

◄ The 14,167-ton *Zeppelin* was launched for Germany's North German Lloyd in June 1914 but was laid up for the duration of the war. She was ceded to Britain in 1919 and managed by White Star. This Cooper card shows her here in the River Mersey in White Star livery.

➤ 'The Ship that brought us home' was probably written on this card by one of the many members of the armed forces scattered across the world after the First World War. The ship's name has also been written along her starboard bow.

The Ship that brought Us Home

◄ Posted on 23 November 1919 to Folkestone, the message on this card reads: *R.M.S. Zeppelin. On sea somewhere. We are having lovely weather. Betty and I have been very sick but are better now. We have 150 children on board so we are not lonely. We get to Gibraltar on Wed. & are stopping 36 hours to get coal. I hope to go ashore. Love Florence.*

➤ *Zeppelin* was sold to Orient Line by the Ministry of Shipping in 1920 for their Australian service and renamed *Ormuz*. The message on this Kingsway card reads: *We are once more on the water, we have a nice roomy ship & a good cabin so hope to have a pleasant voyage. There are a few of our old ship's passengers going back so it's not quite lonely.* North German Lloyd re-purchased her in 1927 and she was renamed *Dresden*. Whilst cruising off the Norwegian coast on 20 June 1934 she struck rocks. The next day she rolled onto her port side and was broken up in situ.

S.15050.   ORIENT LINE S. S. "ORMUZ."

U. S. S. MOBILE

▲ Hamburg-Amerika's *Cleveland* was launched at Hamburg in September 1908 for the transatlantic service. After being laid up for the duration of the First World War, she was taken over by the US Navy as a troop transport and renamed USS *Mobile*. The 16,960-ton vessel is seen here in that capacity on this Muller of New York card. Note the troops swarming over her superstructure.

➤ *Mobile* was chartered from the Shipping Controller by White Star, after she had completed her trooping duties, and she sailed from New York to Liverpool in July 1920. She is seen here being towed from Queenstown after engine trouble on 10 July 1920. Her engines were so unsatisfactory that White Star terminated the charter after only two round-trip transatlantic voyages.

MOBILE.

◀ After three years' Piraeus to New York service for the Byron SS Co. as *King Alexander* the vessel was sold to United America Line in 1923 and reverted to her original name *Cleveland*. The artist Hans Bohrdt illustrates her here on this postcard sporting yellow funnels with grey stripes.

➤ Hamburg-Amerika Line re-purchased the ship in 1926 for their Hamburg–Southampton–New York service. Five years later she was laid up and finally scrapped at Hamburg, in 1933, by her builders Blohm & Voss. This AC Hamburg card carries the postmark 22 June 1929.

Schnelldampfer „Cleveland' (Hamburg-Amerika Linie)

101/2/18 RMS Arabic

▼ The North German Lloyd, twin-screw, 16,786-ton *Berlin* was launched at Bremen in 1908 for the New York–Mediterranean service. At the outbreak of the First World War she was converted into an armed merchant cruiser and minelayer and, as such, laid the mine that sank the battleship HMS *Audacious* in the Irish Sea. Ceded to the Shipping Controller in 1919, she was purchased by White Star in 1920 and we see her here just prior to her handover. In 1921 she was renamed as White Star's third *Arabic*.

▲ *Arabic*, operating White Star's New York–Mediterranean service, was chartered to assist with the final departure of Allied troops from Turkey in October 1923. This Leonar card carries the message: *HMT Arabic with General Harrington on board leaving Constantinople amid hearty cheers from H.M. ships and the evacuation is complete.*

WHITE STAR LINE
S.S. "ARABIC"

THE LARGEST VESSEL REGULARLY EMPLOYED
IN THE MEDITERRANEAN SERVICE

▲ White Star's employment of *Arabic* on their Mediterranean service lasted only until 1924 when, after a fall in passenger numbers due to the introduction of US immigration control, she was switched to the Hamburg–New York service.

RED STAR LINE.

S.S. "ARABIC"
16.786 Tons.

▲ For three years from 1927, *Arabic*, in Red Star Line livery, operated from Antwerp to New York until being sold for scrap at Genoa in 1931.

H.M.T. POLAND

◀ Before being renamed *Poland* in 1920, the *Manitou* of Atlantic Transport Line had been launched as *Victoria* for Wilson's & Furness Leyland Line in 1897. She must, at some time after 1920, have been involved in trooping duties as her title HMT (His Majesty's Transport) suggests. The message on this card stamped 'Received from HM Ships' and postmarked 21 May reads: *13th May My Dear Mum & Dad. Just arrived in Con'sple for six days leave. Weather fine. Hope to have a good time. Yours Bill (Came up on Poland).*

➤ *Poland* was transferred to the White Star Line in 1922 but was laid up after making only three round-trip Bremen–Southampton–Quebec–Montreal voyages. This Kingsway card shows her in White Star Line livery but 'White Star' has been whited out from the wording at the base. *Poland* was scrapped in Italy in 1925 after a three-year lay-up.

S.15107. LINE S. S. "POLAND".

CHAPTER SEVEN

GERMAN GIANTS

R. M. S. HOMERIC.

▲ The 34,351-ton *Columbus*, built for North German Lloyd at Danzig, was 80 per cent complete at the outbreak of the First World War, during which work on her was suspended. Ceded to Britain in 1919, under war reparation agreements, she was purchased by the White Star Line in 1920 and completed under Harland & Wolff's supervision. Renamed *Homeric*, she was delivered from Germany in 1922.

S.S."HOMERIC" JAN 2ⁿ 1923   STEAMING INTO 80 M.P.H GALE.

⌃ Placed on the North Atlantic express service, *Homeric* maintained a three-ship operation with *Olympic* and *Majestic*. Despite being too slow, at 18 knots, *Homeric* had a good reputation as a 'steady ship' in rough seas. She was converted to oil burning the same year as this photograph, 1923.

"S.S. HOMERIC" from BOWS of H·M·S·AJAX· 4·3·23·

▲ After her conversion to oil burning, *Homeric*'s speed was increased to 19.5 knots but she was never to be a profitable vessel owing to her large third-class capacity. She is seen here, outward-bound from Southampton, from the bows of the First World War battleship HMS *Ajax* at Portsmouth.

➤ *Homeric*'s first-class smoking room is illustrated here on a company-issued postcard carrying, on the reverse side, the following advertising: 'The White Star liner "*Homeric*" 34,351 tons is the largest twin-screw steamer in the world and sixth in point of tonnage and is 751ft in length. The "*Homeric*" is one of the popular "BIG THREE" maintaining the Company's Express Mail and Passenger Service between Southampton, Cherbourg and New York which she operates in conjunction with "*Majestic*" and "*Olympic*".'

▼ Another company-issued card, illustrating *Homeric*'s first-class dining saloon with fresh flowers on ready-laid tables.

White Star Line R.M.S. "Homeric"
First Class Smoking Room

White Star Line R.M.S. "Homeric"
First Class Dining Saloon

▼ *Homeric* was switched to cruising from British ports to the Mediterranean in 1932 and passed into Cunard White Star ownership in 1934. Laid up off the Isle of Wight in 1935, she was broken up at Inverkeithing in 1936. This card shows her at Queensferry on 17 June 1936 with her rear funnel already removed.

◄ The launch of Hamburg-Amerika Line's *Bismarck*, at the Blohm & Voss Hamburg yard on 20 June 1914, by the granddaughter of ex-Chancellor Otto von Bismarck. After her unsuccessful attempt, the bottle was broken across the bows by Kaiser Wilhelm II who was also in attendance. At the outbreak of war in August of that year, work on *Bismarck*'s completion was suspended for the duration. The incomplete vessel was ceded to Britain as war reparation in 1919 but suffered serious fire damage in 1920, probably as a result of sabotage.

◄ 1922 and, still named *Bismarck*, ship SS214 is nearing completion under the supervision of a team from Harland & Wolff. At this time she was also converted to oil burning.

▼ The 56,551-ton *Bismarck* sailing to Liverpool from Hamburg in 1922 and after acceptance trials she would pass into White Star ownership as a replacement for the lost *Britannic*, be renamed *Majestic* and become the world's largest liner.

R.M.S. MAJESTIC.

▲ A fine stern view of White Star's second *Majestic* by Ernest Hopkins of Southsea.
Her fastest crossing, in September 1923, was only exceeded by Cunard's *Mauretania*.

R.M.S. " Majestic " (White Star Line)—FITTED BY

THE WELIN DAVIT & ENGINEERING CO., LTD.

5, Lloyd's Avenue, E.C. 3.
Telegrams " QUADAVIT, LONDON."
London Telephone : Royal 0707-08.

624, Royal Liver Building, LIVERPOOL.
48, Avenue Tokio, PARIS.

▲ *Majestic* as featured on an advertising card for the Welin Davit & Engineering Co. Ltd. Her rear funnel was a dummy for ventilation and galley exhausts only.

➤ The United Kingdom did not possess a sufficiently large dry dock to handle a vessel the size of *Majestic* until 1924. She is seen here dry-docked at Boston in November 1922.

R.M.S. MALESTIC
DRY. DOCKED. BOSTON. U.S
NOV. 1922.

▼ *Majestic*'s enormous size is illustrated on this postcard showing her in Southampton's floating dock. The message on the reverse reads: *Here is the Majestic in the floating dock. It will be seen that she is right through the dock, which is not long enough for her, although the dock is 900 feet long. You can only get the photo of the graving dock from the Southern Rly. They won't let anyone else take them or sell them.*

S.S. "Majestic."

C. R. Hoffmann,
1149 Southampton.

White Star Line R.M.S. "MAJESTIC"
The Largest Steamer in the World.
First Class Dining Saloon.

56,621 Tons.

◄ *Majestic*'s first-class dining saloon, the largest ever on a ship, portrayed on a Hoffmann postcard. It is interesting to compare the elegant crystal and table lamps with the tumblers and flowers of *Homeric*'s first-class restaurant. Uptakes, at the side of the ship, to *Majestic*'s first two funnels helped create more spacious public areas.

➤ The á la carte restaurant shown on another Hoffmann postcard. Of White Star's fleet only *Olympic* and *Titanic*, in addition to *Majestic*, featured an á la carte restaurant where first-class passengers were able to dine for an additional fee.

White Star Line R.M.S. "MAJESTIC"
The Largest Steamer in the World.
First Class Restaurant.

56,621 Tons.

2 ND CLASS DINING SALOON, R. M. S. MAJESTIC.

◄ No table lamps or flowers were to be found in the second-class dining saloon. Carafes of water and flat-folded napkins greeted diners here!

➤ The Tourist Third Cabin dining saloon in the latter years of *Majestic*'s career.

WHITE STAR LINE R.M.S. MAJESTIC, 56,551 TONS
THE LARGEST STEAMER IN THE WORLD
TOURIST THIRD CABIN DINING SALOON

White Star Line R.M.S. "MAJESTIC"
The Largest Steamer in the World.
First Class Swimming Bath.

56,621 Tons

◄ *Majestic*'s Roman-style swimming pool, the largest afloat, featured marble benches and columns illustrated on this Hoffmann postcard.

➤ Another Hoffmann card featuring *Majestic*'s popular Palm Court leading to her á la carte restaurant.

White Star Line. R.M.S. "MAJESTIC."
The Largest Steamer in the World.
PALM COURT.

56,551 Tons.

◄ Artistic licence has reduced the size of the tugboat to exaggerate *Majestic*'s enormity on this Regent card produced for the White Star Line. The advertising message on the reverse reads: 'The *Majestic* is a giant liner of the White Star Line, driven by a quadruple screw, with a tonnage of 56,551. She was built at Hamburg and is engaged on the White Star Company's express weekly mail and passenger service between Southampton, Cherbourg and New York. She travels at a speed averaging 25 knots and completes her journey in five and a half days after leaving Southampton. Accommodation is afforded to first, second, tourist third cabin and third-class passengers numbering, in all, 4000.'

R.1389   THE "MAJESTIC" WHITE STAR LINE

LONDON (England)　DUBLIN (Ireland)　PARIS France)

S. S. MAJESTIC
(*World's Largest Ship*)

◄ A White Star Line card issued in the USA and posted from *Majestic* at Plymouth on 13 October 1933. The reverse carries the advertisement: 'Three deluxe modern (*Olympic* was twenty-one!) liners furnish regular express service to Cherbourg and Southampton. *Majestic* (World's Largest Ship), *Olympic* and *Homeric*. Two new cabin liners, *Georgic* and *Britannic* (England's largest motor vessels), with their running mate *Adriatic*, are in regular service from New York and Boston to Cobh and Liverpool'. Within a year White Star had merged with Cunard.

➤ *Majestic*'s stern served as the recreation area for Tourist Third Cabin passengers in this interesting 'thirties' view.

WHITE STAR LINE R.M.S. MAJESTIC, 56,551 TONS
THE LARGEST STEAMER IN THE WORLD
TOURIST THIRD CABIN PROMENADE DECK

HALIFAX FROM THE HARBOUR, HALIFAX, N.S. CANADA. (C.N.R. PHOTO)   MAR. 15

◄ Towards the end of her career, in the summer of 1930, White Star employed *Majestic* on low-cost 'booze' cruises to nowhere as well as from New York to Canada. She is seen here at Halifax NS in this aerial view by Valentine Black from a Canadian National Railways photograph.

➤ After the 1934 merger of White Star and Cunard it was not unusual to see the liveries of both companies featured together. *Majestic*, with Cunard's *Aquitania*, is illustrated by artist Frank Mason (1875–1965) on this postcard used by travel agent Thos. Cook & Son, dated 7 April 1936, to detail part of the Round the World cruise of Cunard's *Franconia* from Hong Kong to Shanghai. Note that small tugs have been used again!

Cunard White Star   *Majestic*

WHITE STAR LINE
TWIN-SCREW R.M.S. "HOMERIC."

▲ Artist William McDowell's (1888–1950) illustration of *Homeric* for the White Star Line on this card posted from Birmingham in 1930. The reverse of the card carries the following wording: 'RMS *Homeric* 34,351 tons. The largest twin screw steamer in the World.'

◀ Cunard White Star featured the unique style of artist James Mann (1883–1946) for this illustration of *Homeric* now in the ownership of the joint organisation.

▼ The two ex-German giants together in Southampton with this stern view of *Majestic* and *Homeric* at the White Star Line berths.

➤ *Majestic* lost her title of 'World's largest Ship' to France's *Normandie* in 1935 and a year later she was laid up at Southampton upon the entry into service of the giant *Queen Mary*. Later that year she was sold to ship breakers Thos. W. Ward but was purchased from them by the Admiralty to serve as a cadet training ship and renamed HMS *Caledonia*. The conversion was carried out by Thornycroft of Southampton prior to her departure on 8 April 1937. She is seen here at her final berth at Rosyth, her masts and funnels having been cut down to enable her to pass under the Forth Railway Bridge.

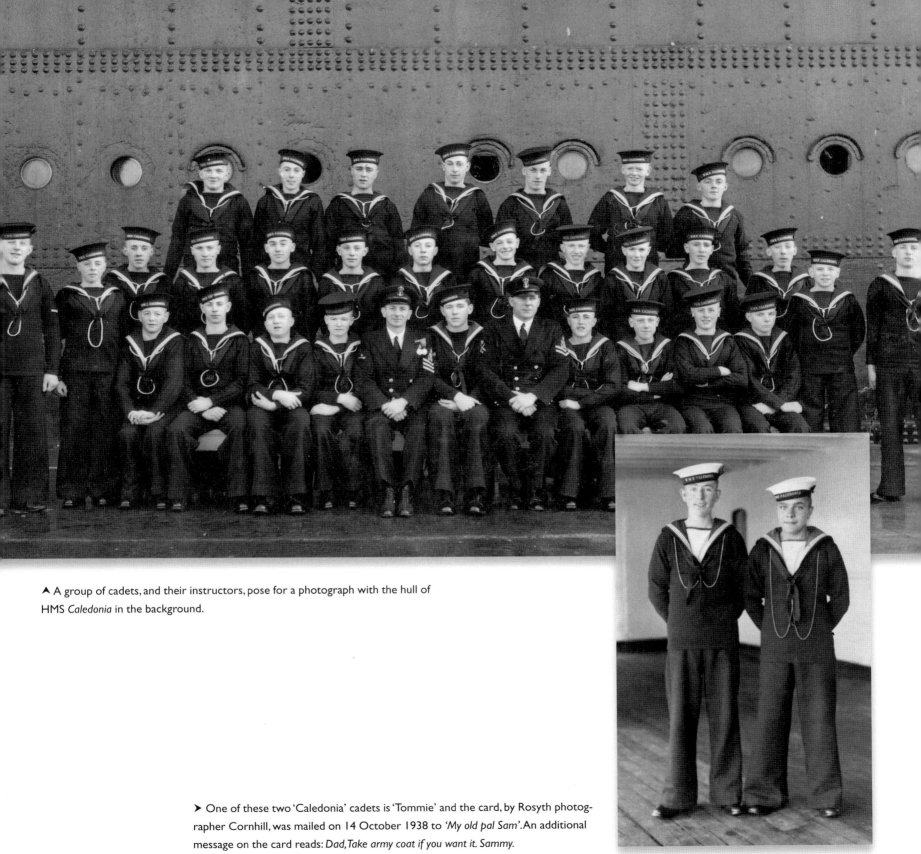

▲ A group of cadets, and their instructors, pose for a photograph with the hull of HMS *Caledonia* in the background.

➤ One of these two 'Caledonia' cadets is 'Tommie' and the card, by Rosyth photographer Cornhill, was mailed on 14 October 1938 to *'My old pal Sam'*. An additional message on the card reads: *Dad, Take army coat if you want it. Sammy.*

◀ A company-issued postcard illustrating *Homeric*'s first-class lounge. The description on the reverse reads: 'Lounge. This fine apartment has the grand air of the Palladian saloons of the eighteenth century. The sunlight scheme of wall and ceiling colour is exhilarating and gay, and the furniture is varied and most inviting.' This particular card has been over-stamped on the reverse by the Coburg Hotel in Tenby for advertising purposes.

▶ *Homeric*'s near-sister *Hindenburg* was laid down at Danzig in 1914 but building work ceased at the outbreak of the First World War and the incomplete vessel was not included in the war reparation demands of 1919. Construction recommenced in 1920 and the liner was launched as *Columbus* (*Homeric*'s original name) in 1922. Operated by North German Lloyd on the transatlantic service she was eventually scuttled by her crew 320 miles off the coast of Virginia in December 1939 to prevent her capture by a British destroyer.

R.M.S. Homeric

Cunard
White Star Line

▲ A White Star Line postcard, with the name 'Cunard' added, illustrating *Homeric* by artist Walter Thomas (1894–1962). Thos. W. Ward, ship-breakers, are using this post-card to advertise the sale of mattresses from the ex-liners *Olympic* and *Homeric*.

◀ Chronologically this, and the subsequent, illustration should have appeared before the views of *Caledonia* as a cadet training ship but have been placed here as they feature the vessel's last voyage. HMS *Caledonia* is seen here on 10 April 1937 passing under the Forth Railway Bridge en route to her final berth at Rosyth.

➤ 10 April 1937 and, escorted by a fleet of tugs, *Caledonia/Majestic* disappears from sight. At the outbreak of the Second World War the cadets were moved to shore accommodation and *Caledonia* was anchored in the Firth of Forth. Sadly, on 29 September 1939, she caught fire and the burnt-out wreck sank at her moorings on an even keel, being finally broken up by Thos. Ward in 1944.

CHAPTER EIGHT

TWILIGHT OF THE IMMC

▲ The *Haverford* was built at John Brown of Clydebank in 1901 for the American Line's Liverpool service to Philadelphia and Boston. After a year of trooping to the Dardanelles during the First World War, she was transferred, within the IMMC, to the White Star Line in March 1921 and is seen here in White Star livery.

▲ Within a year *Haverford* was back with the American Line. This card was posted at Queenstown on 31 August 1921 with the message: *This is a photo of the boat we are now on. The boat started an hour late and we will get to Queenstown, Ireland tomorrow morning. The boat has not begun to rock yet but I guess it will start tomorrow.*

➤ A company-issued card with an illustration by artist Montague Black (1884–1964) showing *Haverford* in White Star Line colours.

WHITE STAR LINE.

TWIN-SCREW S.S. "HAVERFORD," 11,635 TONS.

▼ Another colour card with *Haverford* in American Line colours by Valentine's. Note the 'stand-off' between the two dogs on the quayside. The message on the reverse reads: *Dear Brother & Sister. Just a line to let you know I arrived quite safe after a rather rough voyage. It took me 13 days to come. I think I shall come on faster boat next time. With kindest regards. Fred*

S.S. "Haverford."

WHITE STAR–DOMINION LINE.

TRIPLE-SCREW S.S. "REGINA," 16,500 TONS.

◄ *Regina* illustrated here in Dominion Line colours. She was laid down in 1913 and launched in 1917 at Harland & Wolff in Glasgow, after which she was towed to Belfast for final fitting out. She would be the last vessel to be built for the Dominion Line.

S.S. REGINA

▲ With the closure of the Dominion Line, *Regina* was transferred to White Star service in 1925. This State Series card shows her here in White Star livery.

RED STAR LINE.

TRIPLE-SCREW "WESTERNLAND" 16,500 TONS

▲ *Regina* was again transferred, this time to Red Star Line, in 1929 and renamed *Westernland* a year later. She was never to be converted to oil burning.

Owing to the shortage of merchant shipping at the end of the First World War, *Regina* was hurriedly completed as a troopship with one funnel in 1918. She was employed primarily on the repatriation of troops for the next year.

REGINA 15

> Having been converted to her original design in 1920, *Regina* emerged from Harland & Wolff with two funnels and improved passenger accommodation. The message on this card reads: *We're on our way to Belfast now, haven't long been started as we had to wait for the tide. So far I've got a two-berth cabin to myself but will probably get a partner in tomorrow at Belfast. This is not a very good photo of the boat as it really looks better than in the picture. Would you send the other to Grannie please as I've only got one more stamp.*

R. M. S. REGINA.

R.M.S. "REGINA"

◄ *Regina* here again in White Star colours. Her Topliss davits, which could handle up to twelve boats, are clearly seen on this card by B & A Feilden. This type of davit was probably removed in 1927. The year prior to her transfer to White Star she would be one of the first passenger ships to introduce 'Tourist Class', her third class being improved by more space and better food at a higher fare.

➤ For five years from 1929 *Regina* was employed by Red Star Line as *Westernland* on their trans-atlantic services from Antwerp. She was laid up after Red Star's collapse in 1934, purchased by Arnold Bernstein's short-lived Red Star Line GmbH and then purchased by Holland America Line in June 1939. She later escaped to Britain, after the fall of Holland in 1940, and became the headquarters of the Dutch government in exile. Later converted to a troopship, she was finally scrapped at Blyth in 1947.

735   WESTERNLAND

WHITE STAR—DOMINION LINE.

S.S. "REGINA."   Sept. 8, 1922.

BREAKFAST.
Rolled Oats and Milk
Ling Fish, Cream Sauce
Boiled Eggs
Preserves

Tea   Coffee

DINNER.
Pea Soup
Boiled Cod, Parsley Sauce
Roast Beef, Brown Gravy
Green Peas   Boiled Potatoes
Tapioca Pudding

TEA.
Macaroni, Italienne
Preserved Salmon
Radishes and Spring Onions
Stewed Figs
Tea

SUPPER.
Gruel   Cheese   Biscuits   Cocoa

Any complaint respecting the Food supplied, want of
attention or incivility, should be at once reported to
the Purser or Chief Steward.

WHITE STAR LINE.

R.M.S. "HOMERIC"   12th May, 1923

BREAKFAST.
Rolled Oats with Milk
Fried Tripe
Grilled Sausage   Mashed Potatoes
Fried Bacon
Marmalade   Tea   Coffee

DINNER.
Mock Turtle Soup
Veal Saute Marengo
Roast Lamb - Mint Sauce
Green Peas   Boiled and Roast Potatoes
Roll Jam Pudding
Cabin Biscuits   Cheese

TEA.
Rabbit Pie
Macaroni a l'Italienne
COLD : Pressed Beef   Boiled Ham   Beetroot
Bath Buns   Jam   Tea

SUPPER : Gruel   Biscuits   Cheese   Cocoa
Any complaint respecting the Food supplied, want of
attention, or incivility, should be at once reported to
the Purser or Chief Steward.

⌃ The first in a quartet of third-class menus from the years 1922–23. This very basic 'all day' 8 September 1922 postcard menu for *Regina*, operating on the joint White Star-Dominion Line service to Canada, depicts her Dominion Line work-mate *Canada*.

⌃ Less than a year later, the third-class passengers on *Homeric* enjoy an improved bill of fare on the express service to New York. Note that the passenger has crossed out 'fried' and replaced it by 'stewed' tripe. Could this be a description or a criticism?

WHITE STAR—DOMINION LINE.

Nov. 10, 1923.   s.s. "CANADA."

BREAKFAST.
Scotch Oatmeal with Milk
Fried Plaice
Grilled Country Sausage
Fresh Bread

Jam   Marmalade   Tea   Coffee

DINNER.
Puree of Split Peas
Fricassee of Rabbit
Roast Beef
Carrots and Turnips   Boiled Potatoes
Semolina Pudding
Fresh Fruit

TEA.
Curried Mutton and Boiled Rice
Cold : Roast Beef   Bologna Sausage
Pickles and Beetroot
Stewed Apricots
Tea Cakes

Preserves   Tea

Supper : Cheese   Biscuits   Gruel   Cocoa

Any complaint respecting the Food supplied, want of attention or incivility, should be at once reported to the Purser or Chief Steward.

WHITE STAR LINE.

THIRD CLASS BILL OF FARE,
s.s. "DORIC," Monday, November 12, 1923

BREAKFAST.
Oatmeal Porridge and Milk
Grilled Rump Steak and Onions   Mashed Potatoes
Buttered Eggs for Children
Fresh Bread   Jam   Marmalade
Tea   Coffee

DINNER.
Scotch Broth
Curry and Rice
Roast Mutton, Brown Gravy
Lima Beans   Boiled Potatoes
Semolina Pudding

TEA
Cottage Pie
Cold Roast Beef   Luncheon Sausage   Beetroot
Stewed Fruit   Rock Cakes
Preserves   Tea

SUPPER—Cheese   Biscuits   Cocoa

Any complaint respecting the Food supplied, want of attention, or incivility, should be at once reported to the Purser or Chief Steward.

Good Trip across from Canada

▲ Back to basics with *Canada*'s White Star-Dominion Line menu of 10 November 1923!

▲ Despite the passenger's comment '*Good trip across from Canada*' this Doric menu, of 12 November 1923 illustrating *Adriatic*, makes no mention of the Canadian joint service which continued for a further two years. It would appear, therefore, that White Star supplied stocks of illustrated blank cards to all their vessels, which were then over-printed on board.

R.M.S. PITTSBURGH.   16,322 Tons

◄ The 16,332-ton *Pittsburgh* was laid down at Harland & Wolff, Belfast, in 1913 for the American Line but construction was suspended throughout the First World War and she was finally completed in May 1922 for the White Star Line. As with her sister-ship *Regina*, the rear funnel was a dummy for ventilation purposes only and she sported, initially, the ugly Topliss lifeboat davits as illustrated here on this Ernest Hopkins card posted from Southampton on 10 August 1923.

► *Pittsburgh* was switched to Red Star's transatlantic service from Antwerp in 1926 and her name was changed to *Pennland*. She is shown here still in White Star livery.

Pennland, 16,322 Tons

▼ *Pennland* is seen here in Red Star livery on this Hoffman card, with her Topliss davits having probably been removed in 1926. She continued in Red Star's service until their collapse in 1934.

1130. C. R. Hoffmann, Southampton.

S.S. PENNLAND. 16,322 Tons.

➤ *Pennland* in the funnel colours, thick white bands and red stars, of German ship-owner Arnold Bernstein's Red Star Line GmbH. She, with her sister *Westernland*, was purchased in 1935 after the collapse of the Red Star Line and Bernstein operated the two vessels on the transatlantic service from Antwerp. Bernstein, being Jewish, was arrested under Nazi rule in Germany in January 1937 and accused of breaking foreign exchange regulations. He was fined $400,000 and sentenced to thirty months' imprisonment. Unable to pay the fines, his ships were confiscated and both *Pennland* and *Westernland* were sold to Holland America Line. Bernstein fortunately survived prison, was released in August 1939, fled to the USA and became an American citizen. *Pennland* was chartered by the British as a troopship in 1940 and sunk by German bombers in the Gulf of Athens on 25 April 1941.

∧ A colourful advertisement featuring the joint White Star-Dominion Line service to Canada. *Teutonic* was transferred to this service in 1911 carrying second- and third-class passengers only.

∧ Another Canadian advertisement but featuring, this time, the liner *Albertic* emerging from a 1930 penny coin illustrating the message on the card: 'For less than 1*d* per mile All Found.' The reverse carries the message: '£10 to Canada. For full particulars apply to any White Star Line office or local agents.'

▲ *Doric*, one of White Star's more short-lived ships and depicted here in the unique style of artist James Mann (1883–1946), joined White Star in 1923 to operate their service to Canada. By 1932 the 16,484-ton vessel was laid up for the Canadian winter, employed on Mediterranean cruises from Liverpool in 1933 and continuing summer cruising into Cunard White Star ownership in 1934. On 5 September 1935, returning from a Mediterranean cruise, she collided in fog with the French vessel *Formigny* off Cape Finisterre. Her 700 passengers were transferred to P&O's *Viceroy* of India and Orient Line's *Orion* after she developed a list. Following temporary repairs at Vigo in Spain, it was considered too expensive to repair her and she was scrapped at Cashmore's yard at Newport, Monmouthshire. The ship-breaker has used this postcard to advertise an auction of *Doric*'s fixtures and fittings, which raised £7,500 for the Royal Gwent Hospital. She, and *Vedic*, were the first White Star vessels to have a cruiser stern.

THIS **LINER** WILL BE

OPEN FOR PUBLIC INSPECTION

FROM

FRIDAY 15th TO SATURDAY 23rd NOVEMBER, 1935,

On behalf of the

ROYAL GWENT HOSPITAL

SPECIAL APPEAL FUND.

FIRST AUCTION SALE OF FURNISHINGS will take place on NOVEMBER 26th, 27th, 28th, 29th, 1935.

JOHN CASHMORE Ltd., Shipbreakers, NEWPORT, Mon.

CHAPTER NINE

ROYAL MAIL AND CUNARD

R.M.S.P. "OHIO," TWIN-SCREW (19,000 TONS GROSS). NEW YORK SERVICE.

R. M.S. ALBERTIC. Tonnage 19000

⬥ Royal Mail's *Ohio* was launched in Germany in 1920 as the *Muenchen* for North German Lloyd. She had been laid down in 1914 but work on her was suspended during the First World War. The day after her launch she was ceded to Britain as war reparation and then purchased by Royal Mail Line who renamed her *Ohio*. The 18,940-ton vessel was sold within the Royal Mail Group, to the newly acquired White Star Line in 1927.

⬥ Renamed *Albertic*, the vessel was employed to Canada from Liverpool but switched to London and Southampton in 1929 after the wreck of *Celtic*. Never a great success, the *Albertic* was laid up over the winters of 1930–32. Passing into Cunard White Star ownership in 1934, she became surplus to requirements and was broken up in Osaka.

R.M.S.P. "ORCA," TRIPLE-SCREW (16,063 TONS GROSS). NEW YORK SERVICE.

◄ Royal Mail's *Orca* was launched at Harland & Wolff, Belfast, in 1918 and hurriedly completed for cargo duties. She returned to Harland & Wolff for completion as a passenger ship in February 1921 and Royal Mail employed her from 1923 until 1926 to New York from Southampton. With the acquisition of the White Star Line, *Orca* was transferred and renamed *Calgaric* in 1927.

➤ Royal Mail Line had sold their *Ohio* and *Orca* to the newly acquired White Star Line for £1 million. Both vessels being quite unsuitable, their purchase only contributed to the ever-increasing debt of White Star. *Calgaric*, illustrated here on this B & A Feilden card, operated from Liverpool to Canada but was frequently employed in cruising or else in lay-up. She was chartered for a Scouts and Guides seventeen-day cruise to the Baltic in 1933. Lord and Lady Baden-Powell were on board with a group of 655 and, interestingly, the First Officer on this particular cruise was J.G. Boxall, who had survived the loss of *Titanic* as her Fourth Officer. *Calgaric*, also deemed surplus to requirements after the merger with Cunard, was broken up at Inverkeithing in 1936.

R.M.S CALGARIC.

S. S. LAURENTIC.

◄ The Royal Mail Group, with increasing debt and a looming recession in 1927, was now in serious financial difficulty. In June of that year Harland & Wolff launched the coal-powered *Laurentic* for White Star Line's Canadian service. Low-cost coal was abundantly available in Canada and fast crossings were not essential on the route.

The launch of *Laurentic* had been delayed nine months by the General Strike and she was the first vessel that Harland & Wolff built for the White Star Line on a 'fixed price' contract replacing the usual 'cost plus profit' agreement that had existed between the two companies. The 18,724-ton *Laurentic* operated from Liverpool to Canada from 1928 to 1934 and would be White Star's only ship on the route from 1932.

➤ *Laurentic* was incorporated into the joint fleet after the merger with Cunard and is shown here, in another James Mann illustration, with her White Star flag flying above that of Cunard on the mainmast. This flag positioning was reversed on Cunard's vessels. Employed mainly on low-cost cruising (£1 per day) in 1935, *Laurentic* spent the following years predominantly in lay-up until the outbreak of the Second World War when she was acquired by the Admiralty and converted into an armed merchant cruiser. On 3 November 1940 she was torpedoed and sunk by U-boat ace Otto Kretschmer's U99 off Co. Donegal with the loss of forty-nine lives.

Cunard White Star   *"Laurentic"*

▲ A self-explanatory advertisement on this Horrocks & Co. card. The 1930s gentle-man appears very pleased with his acquisition!

▲ Another colourful postcard, this time advertising White Star's Mediterranean services. Once again *Albertic* appears to be the vessel featured on this card by Alfieri & Lacroix.

WHITE STAR LINE CANADIAN SERVICE

S. S. "REGINA"   16,500 TONS EACH   S. S. "DORIC"

⌃ With the demise of the Dominion Line in 1926 came a change of name to White Star Line Canadian Service as reflected on this postcard featuring the near-identical *Regina* and *Doric*. White Star's Canadian offices are using this card to promote the company's departures to the UK. Note that the service is weekly and operated by a different vessel each time. The year of issue is not specified and 'Scotch' customers may have questioned the use of this particular name!

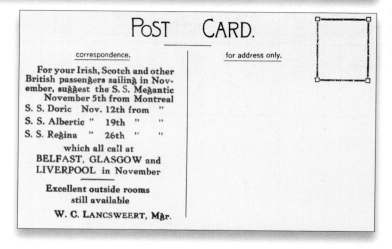

POST CARD.

correspondence.   for address only.

For your Irish, Scotch and other British passengers sailing in November, suggest the S. S. Megantic November 5th from Montreal
S. S. Doric Nov. 12th from "
S. S. Albertic " 19th " "
S. S. Regina " 26th " "
which all call at
BELFAST, GLASGOW and LIVERPOOL in November

Excellent outside rooms still available

W. C. LANCSWEERT, Mgr.

"M.V. BRITANNIC"   JUNE 1930

▲ Huge debt and the Depression had forced White Star's abandonment of the planned super-liner *Oceanic* but two smaller motor vessels were ordered from Harland & Wolff, Belfast. The first of these, White Star's third *Britannic*, is seen here at Liverpool, on this A.P. Goodman card, having arrived from Belfast prior to her maiden voyage to New York. She departed on Saturday 28 June 1930. The 26,943-ton *Britannic* was, when launched in August 1929, the second-largest motor-ship in the world. Her forward funnel was a dummy housing the radio cabin, engineers' lounge and water tanks.

◀ A company-issued card promoting *Britannic*'s 'Cabin Card Room', posted at Worcester in May 1932. The advertisement on the reverse reads: 'The Card Room is a delightful apartment in the French Gothic style, influenced, in certain details, by the renaissance, but retaining, in the carved panelling, the arched fireplace and rich colouring, the characteristics of a medieval room.' The only visible card table would accommodate four players. *Britannic*'s Cabin class could hold up to 504 passengers!

▶ Another company-issued card, this time featuring *Britannic*'s 'Cabin Dining Saloon'. On the reverse is written: 'The Dining Saloon, in the style of Louis XIV, is two decks high. A feature is made of the lighting which, in the centre part of the room, is mainly concealed, flooding the whole of the upper part with a soft glow and adding to the apparent height.'

M.V. BRITANNIC
LUBRICATED THROUGHOUT BY W. B. DICK & CO., LTD.

◄ A company-issued postcard, featuring an image of *Britannic* by artist William McDowell (1888–1950), used by W.B. Dick & Co. as an advertisement. Up until the merger with Cunard in 1934 *Britannic* had sailed from Liverpool to New York, via Belfast and Glasgow, with occasional winter cruises from New York to the West Indies but in 1935 she was switched to the London–Le Havre–Southampton–New York service. At the outbreak of the Second World War she was converted for trooping and served throughout the war, transporting over 180,000 troops and covering over 376,000 miles.

➤ *Britannic* returned to Harland & Wolff, Belfast for her post-war refit in 1947, during which her Promenade Deck was glazed in and her tonnage increased to 27,650. 'White Star' has been dropped by Cunard on this card, probably issued in 1957, posted from Cobh on 2 June. The message reads: *Dear Mother. I'm sending this card from the Britannic. Mable and I have just had our lunch. It's 2.15pm Frid., we sail in about half an hour, it's a lovely day and all's well. Will write you from the other side. Love Janet.*

Britannic's last sailing was from New York on 2 December 1960 for Liverpool and she was scrapped at Inverkeithing in 1961. With her departure the only remaining ex-White Star vessels afloat were the *Athenic*, unrecognisable as the whaler *Pelagos* broken up in 1962, and the tender *Nomadic*, a floating restaurant in Paris on the River Seine.

Cunard M.V. "Britannic"

M.V. "GEORGIC."

◄ *Georgic*, second of the two motor vessels, was identifiable by her rounded bridge, that of her sister *Britannic* being straight sided. Unlike *Britannic*'s interiors, those of *Georgic* were more art deco in style. Sadly no postcards of *Georgic*'s public rooms appear to be available. From 1932 until the outbreak of war *Georgic* and *Britannic* shared similar careers. *Georgic*'s conversion to troopship, with a capacity of 3,000, was complete by April 1940. During a bomb attack by German aircraft in the Gulf of Suez in 1941 she was hit twice and badly damaged by fire and exploding ammunition. The salvaged vessel returned to Belfast, via Karachi and Bombay, in February 1943.

➤ His Majesty's Transport *Georgic*, now owned by the Ministry of Transport, emerged in 1944 with one funnel and a short foremast to continue her trooping duties until 1948.

HIS MAJESTY'S TRANSPORT "GEORGIC."

S.S. GEORGIC.

▲ *Georgic* was refitted in 1948 and, in White Star Line colours, operated 'assisted passage' emigrant services to Australia and New Zealand with occasional charters to Cunard for New York service in the early fifties. The message carried on this card, posted at Southampton on 11 November 1953, reads: *WED. We thought you might like to see the boat we are travelling in. Very good accommodation & excellent food. We sail at mid-day today. Just going to prepare for boat station drill. Our very kindest regards. Capt. & Mrs. W. Stewart. Georgic's* last voyage was in 1955 as a troopship from Hong Kong to Liverpool and she was scrapped at Faslane in 1956, the last liner to be built for the White Star Line.

END NOTE

The newly formed Cunard-White Star Line was registered on 10 May 1934 with Cunard holding 62 per cent and White Star 38 per cent of the shares. White Star Line Ltd, formed after the Royal Mail purchase from IMMC, was wound up with debts of over £11 million on 8 April 1935 and OSNC dissolved on 21 August 1939.

Cunard purchased the 38 per cent shareholding of OSNC in 1947 and on 31 December 1949 the Cunard Steamship Company took over all the activities of Cunard-White Star. The famous White Star Line had ceased to exist.

BIBLIOGRAPHY

White Star by Roy Anderson (T. Stephenson & Sons Ltd, 1964)

Merchant Fleets in Profile 2: The Ships of the Cunard, American, Red Star, Inman, Leyland, Dominion, Atlantic Transport and White Star Lines by Duncan Hawes (Patrick Stephens Ltd. ISBN 0 85059 324 7)

The White Star Line – An Illustrated History 1869–1934 by Paul Louden-Brown (The *Titanic* Historical Society. ISBN 1 903374 00 6)

Ships of the White Star Line by Richard de Kerbrech (Ian Allan Publishing Ltd. ISBN 978 0 7110 33665)

A Postcard History of the Passenger Liner by Christopher Deakes (Chatham Publishing. ISBN 1 86176 224 0)

INDEX